Frank Arjava Petter

Reiki Fire

New Information about the Origins of the Reiki Power
A Complete Manual

LOTUS LIGHT
SHANGRI-LA

1st English Edition 1997
2nd printing 1997, 3rd revised edition 1998
4th printing 2000
© by Lotus Light Publications
Box 325, Twin Lakes, WI 53181, USA
The Shangri-La Series is published in cooperation
with Schneelöwe Verlagsberatung, Federal Republic of Germany
© 1997 by Windpferd Verlagsgesellschaft mbH, Aitrang, Germany
Edited by Marton Radkai
Cover design by Kuhn Grafik, Digitales Design, Zurich
by using a picture of Mikao Usui by Tsutomu Oishi
Photographs: Frank Arjava Petter and Tsutomu Oishi (page 23)
Illustrations: Ute Rossow

ISBN 0-914955-50-0
Library of Congress Catalog Number 97-71444

Printed in USA

Table of Contents

*I titled this book Reiki Fire because Reiki energy
consumes all duality in its purity.*

*Dedicated to Osho
In loving gratitude*

Preface

Sometimes it happens that a book is urgently needed and events constellate to bring together the right people at the appropriate time in a suitable way. Something like this happened with the present work.

Ever since I have been involved in Reiki, the story of how this healing art originated has interested me. However, despite all my efforts it had only been possible for me to find indirect research on sources, to read, compare, and question travelers, yet, so much has remained a secret and in the realm of unconfirmable speculation. Just when I was ready to throw in the towel and console myself with the idea of perhaps planning a longer trip to Japan in ten years or so, I was invited to Berlin for a podium discussion on Reiki by an esoteric magazine.

During the preparatory discussions with the organizer, he told me about a German Reiki Master who lives in Japan and has been researching the history of the Usui System of Natural Healing with great dedication. I asked him for the address and then simply called the telephone number. In a lengthy conversation, I sensed that there was something quite kindred between myself and this person who had been a stranger to me up to that day. I had the feeling that we had already known each other for years. The time passed rapidly because he had such fascinating things to say about his research. He had even written a book in which he discussed it, among other things, but couldn't find a publisher for it in Japan.

"Well," I thought to myself, "maybe not in Japan ... but in Gemany there's the Windpferd Publishing Company, which has always been very supportive of such projects." The contacts were soon made, and today I am permitted to write the preface to this book. In my opinion, it is by far the most important book on the topic of Reiki in recent years. Frank Arjava Petter knows how to write in an exciting, sensitive, and absorbing way. His devotion to Reiki and abundant experience with the spiritual path can be felt on every page.

Even if it didn't publicize pioneer findings on the history of the Usui System of Natural Healing's origins, this would still be one of the best books on the topic.

During the good half of a year in which the text was translated from English into German, almost every month Frank Arjava Petter came up with additional important and brand-new research results that increasingly rounded off the book. I am fascinated here by the figure of Dr. Usui, who has emerged in a totally unusual way for the most part. On the one hand, he is clearly no longer the magical, practically superhuman figure who appears to be perfect, but in another sense he gains immensely in human stature, and I find him much more likeable than back when it was only possible to learn something about him through strongly stylized stories that were passed on by word of mouth.

Dr. Usui was certainly familiar with despair and defeat as a result of his own experiences. Yet, he also learned from life and let something great and beautiful grow from it, namely his Usui System of Natural Healing. As a person who had traveled much, read a great deal, and was interested in everything related to human happiness and spirituality, he developed the Reiki System and passed it on to thousands of people in Japan. Years after his death, this subtle art of healing reached the West.

Unfortunately, essential information about its history and versatility had been lost along the way. This has now been brought to full circle by a Westerner, who also can't resist doing research and has contributed important components to completing Dr. Usui's legacy. This is immensely significant at the current time in particular because it means that the discussion on the nature of "authentic Reiki," which has been largely based on beliefs and prejudices up to now, can be ended for the most part. Traditional Reiki, as Dr. Usui employed it, apparently has such versatility and tremendous spiritual content that it can be the homeland of an enormous range of individual expressions. And yet, the true essence of Reiki has now also become more clear than it has ever been.

I hope that this book by Frank Arjava Petter will soon be followed by others from his pen with the same high level of excitement and information. There are not many authors who can combine the heart and the mind so well in what they write.

I wish this book what it unconditionally deserves in my opinion: many, many interested readers throughout the world who let themselves become inspired in their approach to Reiki by it.

Walter Lübeck

Walter Lübeck

Reiki Master and author of
The Complete Reiki Handbook

Introduction
and Reiki History

Prologue

My life was meaningless until the day in March 1979 when I set out to rescue my brother from what appeared to be the clutches of an obscure guru in India. My meeting with Osho Rajneesh in Poona for the first time was the decisive event in my life up to that point. Instead of "rescuing" my brother, I myself was rescued! Ever since the day I was accepted as his disciple, every moment has been a great adventure, and writing this book about Reiki has been very rewarding. It has given me the chance to delve deeper into myself and gain greater clarity. I hope the readers will find inspiration here, whether they are already familiar with Reiki or not.

I would like to add that I do not claim any originality for "my" thoughts, since all thoughts are in fact the collective treasure of humankind. I have gained many insights thanks to the guidance of my spiritual master Osho and many others, it would be impossible to list and thank them all.

Thank you, thank you, thank you!

About My Life

I was born on August 24th, 1960 in Düsseldorf, Germany, the second son of Rosemarie and Hans-Georg Petter. My two grandmothers were of ancient German aristocratic descent. Through my paternal grandmother Charlotte von Bismarck, I am related to the German statesman and chancellor Otto von Bismarck. On the maternal side I am the great-grandson of the famous scientist and writer Ferdinand von Raesfeld. For as long as I can remember, I have been exposed to nobility, its grace and magnanimity.

I first encountered meditation when I was 4 or 5 years old. A friend of my maternal grandmother, a student of the German mystic Rudolf Steiner, suddenly said to my brother and me: "Please don't mind me, I'm going to look stupid now for a while, so just go on about your business." She then closed her eyes and meditated. This was the first time I was introduced to nobility of the heart instead of nobility of the blood. This experience left a powerful impression on me. I treasured it within throughout my blissful childhood.

About 10 years later, I had my second encounter with meditation. While attending high school, I developed a chronic 24-hour stomach ache obviously caused my the stress of attending school. Doctors and hospitals failed to find a cure. Eventually, after our family doctor had passed away, my mother found a new doctor in the phone book whose name was the same as the doctor who had tended to her when she was a child in Wroclaw, Poland. As it turned out, he was the son of my mother's childhood doctor and a student of the German Zen-teacher Karlfried von Dürkheim. After a few consultations, he suggested that I learn meditation. Because of my youth, he thought it best to start with a more physical approach, namely autogenic training (as described in chapter Meditation). I complied, and was soon learning from a Düsseldorf psychiatrist, whose name I have unfortunately forgotten.

About one year later, I began learning Raja Yoga under the supervision of Mr. S. Dutta Roy, a friend's father, and a man with very magnetic energy. Around that time I decided that after finishing school, I would secretly pack up my bags and leave for Japan, where I would become a Zen monk and live happily ever after. I was in for a great surprise.

At 18 I went to Poona, India to rescue my brother who had fallen prey to an obscure Indian guru.

Due to my practice of yoga, I was thoroughly convinced of my own purity and austerity, and was sure I could persuade him to return with me back to Germany.

My family was happy to pay for my trip to India, so off I went. On the flight from Frankfurt to Bombay I happened to sit next to a wealthy Nepalese businessman from Bhaktapur. He invited me to change my plans and come with him to Nepal to marry his daughter, who was traveling with him. She was very beautiful indeed, but I did have another task to take care of. I thanked the man and went to Poona. Upon entering the "Gateless Gate" of the Rajneesh ashram (now known as Osho Commune International), I received the shock of my life: I found myself in the midst of 5000 spiritual seekers who were at least as "pure and austere" as I had thought myself to be. I soon realized that under the guidance of a master the work we do on ourselves increases a thousandfold, and I promptly became a disciple of Osho. Life suddenly turned topsy-turvy. Instead of bringing my wayward brother back to Europe, I returned to my parents' house alone, sold everything I owned, and within a short while was back in India to stay "forever." After a few months attending various therapy and meditation groups, I started to work in the ashram, growing the master's food.

About two years later, Osho's Commune moved to the USA, and I followed in 1983. I became a farmer again, spending almost three years at Rajneeshpuram in Oregon. When the commune dissolved, I left for Europe and worked a variety of odd jobs until I met my wife Chetna M. Kobayashi at my next visit to Poona in 1988. After working for six months in the master's garden and helping with security in his house, we took off on a three-year trip around the world. The first leg of the journey, if you will, included Thailand, Singapore, Indonesia, Nepal, India and then Germany and

Austria. The following year took us to Japan. Instead of becoming a Zen monk as I had once wanted to, I became an English teacher. However, after several months in Sapporo we packed up again and went to America where the grass seemed greener. In fact it wasn't: It was a period of bear survival, culminating in the Gulf War, so we left once again, first to Europe and then back to India.

Once in India, we decided to go back to Japan and start a language school. We arrived in Sapporo in August 1991 with $200, no job and no connections. After two weeks we found a house to rent and borrowed the money for deposits and the like from Chetna's family. Soon afterwards, I was offered several jobs but turned them down.

The following winter, we started preparing our business and went to a bank where we didn't even have an account to ask for a loan. Against all odds, the bank gladly accepted our proposal. We started our school which is still thriving to this day.

In the winter of 1992, I went to Berlin to learn Reiki for my own personal growth. I had been interested in Reiki for many years already, but somehow had always missed the chance of being initiated.

I had not intended to teach Reiki in Japan, but about five month after my return from Europe, life suddenly took a different turn. In April 1993, we started teaching all Reiki degrees, including the Teacher's Degree. At that time only the first two degrees were available to the public. Many people who had already learned the first or the second degree flocked to Sapporo from all over Japan. We've been busy teaching ever since.

We only do individual initiations. For appointments please contact us at the address given on page 126.

Introduction

Throughout history, humankind has often turned to spirituality in times of distress. Now, on the brink of totally destroying this beautiful playground, many people are turning to higher agencies for guidance, and some are turning inwards. There are many ways to aim the arrow of awareness towards your own center, and Reiki is just one of them. It is a perfect self-help system that adjusts to the user and requires no medium, regardless of whether you are a newcomer to the inner world, a hard-boiled intellectual, a body-oriented yoga student, a housewife or a devotee. It puts us back in touch with the long-forgotten but all-pervading life energy and teaches us how to love ourselves again. It helps us bridge the man-made gap between our fellow human beings and nature, so we can all live in harmony again. For some, Reiki is one of many forms of bodywork, for others it is an alternative New-Age healing art, and still for others it is a meditation technique. It all depends on the practitioner's viewpoint.

Writing a book on Reiki is a cosmic joke, like chasing your own shadow. It is present wherever and whatever we may be, yet evades our intellectual judgment the moment we turn our head to look at it. All over the world healers work with life energy, which can be compared to a family with many members. Every form of life energy has its own "individuality," its own characteristics, but they are all made of the same fundamental material. Called *prana* in India, *elan vital* in Europe, *chi* in China, *orgone* by W. Reich, and *ki* in Japan (just to mention a few of its names), Reiki is the energy that pervades everything sentient and insentient. It is ever-changing, yet always the same. In the eyes of Reiki, everything is alive and therefore worthy of respect: from the rocks in your garden to the hand of your beloved in yours ...

According to Indian, Tibetan, and Chinese philosophy, and now modern science too, we are surrounded by an incredibly lively universe that is made up of energy. Scientists have recently demonstrated that what used to be thought of as "solid" matter is in fact rapidly moving energy particles. Solidity is an illusion caused by the limitation of our perception. Everything is energy and, therefore, alive and receptive to energy.

Even though we are floating in this pool of refreshing, life-giving energy 24 hours a day, we have forgotten its presence and can no longer grasp its positive effects on our physical and psychological health. Maybe it is easier to describe Reiki by stating what it is not: It is neither yours nor mine, neither old nor young, neither good nor bad.

It is cosmic evolution, and it is the womb that surrounds us. Initiation into Reiki does not necessarily turn you into a great healer, wealthy businessman, or luminous being. It simply brings out the best in you, intensifies your capabilities, and shows you what parts of your life have not yet been integrated.

Reiki also reveals the path to relaxation, which is so important in our busy lives. Without it, we forget how precious every single moment of our fleeting existence really is. Technically speaking, Reiki is one of many methods that are part of the Chinese family of Qigong and are used to activate, harmonize, and reconnect the self with the universal energy. It has its roots in ancient Buddhism/Shintoism, but differs from the common streams in one central point: the energy is transferred or made available to the student by initiation, not by years of long practice. You could call it the lazy man's Qigong.

Anyone can become a Reiki channel in a matter of a day or two. No skill and no special preparations or degrees are necessary. It is our birthright. Once initiated into Reiki, a person remains a Reiki channel throughout his or her lifetime, even if it isn't put to use. Of course, daily practice deepens understanding of the universal life force and also helps become a clear channel for it. There is no philosophy or religion attached to it, it is pure energy! Reiki treatment is safe in any situation irrespective of disease or discomfort, but it is no substitute for professional medical care. Reiki can be easily combined with orthodox medicine, as well as with alternative healing or relaxation methods. It's about time that orthodox and alternative healing methods work hand-in-hand instead of competing.

The Reiki system is divided into three, or some cases four, degrees that are like building blocks. An individual does not have to complete the whole curriculum. In fact, many people the world round have learned only the first or the first two degrees. However, the sequence of the degrees has to be followed. Each degree is complete in itself. The chapter "The Degrees" gives more information on this topic.

Understanding Reiki in its totality is an endless process. Reading a book or two and gathering information will not suffice. Reiki cannot be conveniently described, nor can its effects on you be determined in a guidebook. As long as you live, however, you will experience continuous personal growth. The best thing to do is go with the flow and trust that life itself will shower its blessings upon you. The rest is every individual's personal mystery.

When talking about "energy" and metaphysics, I have purposely abstained from trying to scientifically explain the inexplicable. The attempt at scientific demystification is just another trick of the (tiny) rational part of our mind to keep maintain its supremacy as sole ruler of our lives. Existence is and remains forever a mystery, and should be celebrated in those terms.

In this spirit, I wish you all the best that life has to give, whatever that means for you. I hope you will enjoy this book and draw inspiration from it.

Reiki History

Generally speaking, there are five different streams of the Chinese Qigong that have traveled throughout the world. They all originated in either Taoism, Buddhism, or Confucianism and are divided into active, active/passive, and passive styles. In Chinese terminology they are called yin, yin/yang and yang styles. Yin refers to the passive, female aspects of ourselves and our surroundings, like the moon. The Chinese character for yin means "the shadow side" and the character for yang means "the light side." Yang refers to the male aspects of ourselves and our surroundings, like the sun.

The most common Qigong stream in both East and West is probably the wide range of martial arts that employ mostly physical exercises to strengthen body and mind in order to make them resistant in the event of physical or moral attack. They have also served as physical exercises for monks who spend the better parts of their lives meditating and not giving enough attention to their bodies.

The second category are strictly medical Qigong exercises, which are very common in China and have recently become popular in Japan as well. They are meant to combat disease and make the practitioner exceedingly healthy by storing vital energy in the lower abdomen. They also aim at prolonging life. Like the martial arts, the medical Qigong exercises belong to the yang streams.

Confucian Qigong belongs to the yin stream and aims mainly at calming the mind, making it receptive to moral wisdom. Taoist Qigong exercises are both active and passive, employing an array of breathing exercises, internal massage, visualization and physical exercises in order to help the practitioner back to perfect balance of body, mind and soul.

Buddhist Qigong exercises belong to the yin stream because their main focus lies on the expansion of inner awareness. Physical balancing is a welcome by-product, but not the primary goal. Some Tibetan Buddhist Qigong techniques help practitioners exercise their bodies by mere visualization. They do not have to move at all!

Both Taoist and Buddhist Qigong exercises also aim at strengthening the body in order to help the practitioner physically survive spiritual enlightenment, which can be a very powerful experience. The Indian saint Ramana Maharshi compared enlightenment to "an elephant trying to enter a tiny bamboo hut."

Reiki is one of the Buddhist offspring of Qigong with added Shintoist influence. It was rediscovered by Mr. Mikao Usui of Kyoto, Japan, toward the end of the 19th century. It was he who named it "Rei-Ki."* In Japanese the character Rei stands for holy, spirit, mystery, gift, nature spirit, or invisible spirit, and the character Ki means energy, nature scene, talent and feeling. Usually Reiki is translated as "universal life energy." Even though Mr. Usui wasn't a doctor in the conventional sense of the word, I will refer to him as Dr. Usui since he was a doctor in the real sense of the word, i.e., he made it his life's work to heal other people's body and mind. In the old days in Japan his students called him Usui-sensei , which means teacher.

Dr. Usui's biography is clouded and filled with mysteries. Much of the so called "Japanese" information circulated about him and his movement outside of Japan, has either been blown out of proportion or not properly researched. The kanji for Reiki was very often misspelled. Almost all German and English Reiki books, for instance, claim that Dr. Usui was the principal of Doshisha University in Kyoto and later studied at the University of Chicago. Archivists at both institutes told us on the telephone that a Mikao Usui had neither enrolled in any of their classes nor taught at either school. In several books the original Usui Reiki movement, which is called Usui Shiki Ryoho is referred to as "Usui Shiko Ryoho". The Japanese word "shiki" means style, form or system. The word "shiko" means urine!

Fact is, however, that Usui-san was honored for his good deeds by the Meiji Emperor of Japan, but so were thousands of others every year.

---

*There is no equivalent sound for "R" in Japanese. It is pronounced "Lay-Key".

Most sources claim that Dr. Usui was a Christian. I have not been able to find any proof of this in his teachings. My theory is that the seemingly Christian aspects of Reiki were added in America to make Reiki more easily acceptable to Christian countries. However, according to my friend and translator Lynn Wakisaka-Evans, it is possible that Dr. Usui may have embraced Christianity for a brief period during his inner search. Dr. Usui is supposed to have worked in the slums healing beggars, a very Christian notion.

I believe, that he went out to heal the victims of the great Kanto earthquake that devastated Tokyo in 1923. Even if he favored Christianity, it does not mean that he was a Christian in the classical sense.

Until the Meiji period, Japan had deliberately isolated itself from the rest of the world. Then, quite suddenly, it opened up its horizons to Western ideas. Progressive intellectuals felt that being involved in anything foreign was very attractive.

The thirst for Western culture has not yet been quenched in Japan. Fast-food restaurants and game centers have been built next to ancient Shinto shrines and kimono stores. On the surface it seems that East and West have finally met, but on closer examination, we find that they are only co-existing. Westerners usually think of Japan as the country of Za Zen, cherry blossoms and cleanliness. But the foreigner who enters Japan for the first time is prone to experience a severe culture-shock. The fact is that religion and, to some extent, the family have been replaced by corporate society. Religiousness has become a pro forma affair.

The funniest and most bizarre anecdote of how East and West get mixed up in "religious" ceremonies in Japan was told to me recently by a friend, Ms. N. One of her friends, who happens to be a Buddhist monk, invited her to his marriage. When the N's arrived at the reception, they found the priest with his head shaven and wearing a white tuxedo in the middle of a "Christian" marriage ceremony. Another example clearly illustrates the current state of affairs: Recently a large church was built in our neighborhood for the sole purpose of conducting marriages. But it has neither a priest, nor a congregation!

„Japanese" religions are treated in similar fashion. Most contemporary Japanese families follow both main religions, Buddhism and Shintoism, for convenience sake if they can afford to do so. Japanese Buddhism is not accepted as truly Buddhist in some traditionally Buddhist countries.

Usually every Japanese celebrates a Shinto birth ceremony, a Shinto/Christian marriage, and a Buddhist funeral. That way, all the gods are satisfied.

Officially, 0.7% of the population (1,537,725 people) adheres to Christianity; 40.4% (89,748,700 people) to Buddhism; and 53.8% (118,185,150 people) to Shintoism; 5.1% (11,203,425 people) to other religions. The funny thing is that if you add up the official numbers, you get a total population of 220 million, and Japan only has 120 million inhabitants! Actually, at least 70% of the population should be classified as "non-religious" in the Western sense of the word.

The Western Reiki Movement

Most Reiki teachers describe the Western movement as follows: Before his death, Dr. Usui passed his knowledge on to several others and made Mr. Chujiro Hayashi, a commander in the Imperial Navy of Japan, the Reiki grand master with the responsibility of leading all the other Reiki teachers. It was he who brought Reiki from Japan to the USA when he visited Hawaii at the end of 1936 to meet with one of his students, Hawayo H. Takata. Ms. Takata was a "nikkeijin" (the Japanese word "nikkeijin" means a Japanese immigrant living abroad) born on the island of Kauai, Hawaii on December 24th, 1900.

Just how many people received the Reiki master title from Dr. Hayashi is unknown, but we do know that he made Ms. Takata a Reiki master when he visited Hawaii in 1938. Just before his death on May 10th, 1941 he declared Ms. Takata Reiki Grand Master and head of the Reiki movement.

Ms. Takata reportedly declared that in 1941 there were only five living Reiki Masters under her leadership. She, in turn, is reported to have granted 22 masterships before her death on December 12th, 1980, and she willed the title of Grand Master to her granddaughter, Phyllis Lei Furumoto. After Ms. Takata's death, the Western Reiki movement split into two directions: the "Reiki Alliance" led by Phyllis Furumoto and the "The Radiance Technique" led by Ms. Barbara Ray and based in the USA. Several other Reiki branches grew out of the "Reiki Alliance," such as the independent Reiki Masters (our line) and Osho Reiki.

The Japanese Reiki Movement

So far we have gathered information on two Reiki streams in Japan. The first one is in Tokyo, the second one in Shizuoka prefecture in the state of Chubu, south of Tokyo.

At the beginning of 1993, my wife Chetna interviewed one of Dr. Usui's relatives, the wife of his grandson, who told us that her mother-in-law, Dr. Usui's daughter, had left a clause in her will stating that his name should never be mentioned in her house! By the time she married, Dr. Usui was already dead. Consequently, she didn't know much about her grandfather-in-law at all and in fact seemed annoyed that we had brought up this sore spot in the family history. She wrote to us later saying she was not permitted to talk about the matter and asked us not to bother her anymore, which we naturally respected. Apparently, several people had called her in the past few years to inquire about Reiki history. One person even called from abroad, but she didn't say whether he was a foreigner or a Japanese national living outside Japan.

A little earlier that year, one of our students had given us the phone number of the Usui Reiki Ryoho Gakkai in Tokyo. The person who answered the phone asked us not to publish her name. She said that she did not intend to read my book and didn't want anything to do with Reiki "that comes from outside of Japan!" She also mentioned that she had been approached by a Japanese individual who teaches Reiki in New York, but had refused to meet that person. However, she kindly shared the following information regarding Dr. Usui with us:

21

Mikao Usui was born on August 15th (1865) in the village of Yago, which is situated in the Yamgata district of the Gifu prefecture, southern Japan. He was married to Sadako Suzuki and had two children. He died on March 9th, 1926, of a stroke, after having recovered from two previous ones two years before. He is buried at Saihoji temple, a Buddhist temple in the suburbs of Tokyo. His wife and son are also buried there. You will find a photograph of his grave and memorial on page 24.

When we contacted the temple, we found out that it is not a Zen temple, but that it belongs to mainstream Buddhism.

As we learned from the inscription on Dr. Usui's tombstone (you will find a translation of it on page 28), he taught Reiki to about 2000 people. There were Reiki centers and Reiki clinics in many parts of the country. Workshops by Dr. Usui and his chief disciples were conducted on a regular basis. The following information was shared with us by Mr. Tsutomu Oishi, a gentleman in his late sixties from Shizuoka City. He received healing sessions from Ms. Shizuko Akimoto at her clinic in Tokyo. She had acquired the Reiki Teachers Degree from us and was not aware of the fact that Mr. Oishi had learned Reiki from one of Dr. Usui's chief disciples about 40 years ago!

Mr. Oishi's mother had learned the so-called middle degree (Second Reiki Degree?) when he was a little child. He asked her about it often, but she always replied that she had promised not to discuss it. Mr. Oishi's brother had had polio, and his mother treated him regularly until he was completely healed.

Encouraged by her success, she went out and treated all the polio stricken children in the neighborhood.

During the past 30 years, Mr. Oishi had no longer any contact with Reiki, but recently he had started thinking about it again. In August 1995, he met Ms. Akimoto not knowing that she was a Reiki practitioner, and suddenly said to her during one of the healing sessions: "You know, there is a natural healing technique called Reiki." Ms. Akimoto was thrilled, since many of us had been researching Reiki history for years with very little success.

In several meetings Mr. Oishi then told her what he knew of Dr. Usui and the Reiki movement in Shizuoka. I carefully

Mikao Usui*

---

* In the top left corner of the photograph you see the five Reiki principles written by Dr. Usui himself.

above:
In the middle
Usui´s gravestone
at the right side
his memorial
stone

Memorial stone at Usui´s grave

sifted through the information, and what follows is an account of what I thought fit for publication in a book. The photograph of Dr. Usui on page 23 has been graciously provided by Mr. Oishi. It was taken while Dr. Usui was conducting a workshop in Shizuoka. The exact date is unknown. At this point I would like to thank Mr. Oishi from the bottom of my heart for his generosity in sharing his knowledge and the wonderful photograph of Dr. Usui with all of us!

The story of Reiki is as follows: Dr. Usui had once run a business that failed. It left him not only with a great debt load, but also with the desire to seek something other than material gain. Dr. Usui used to meditate at a waterfall on Mt. Kurama (see photograph on page 116). One day, while standing under the waterfall, he had a satori.*

Sometime after his experience on Mount Kurama, Dr. Usui founded the "Usui Reiki Ryoho Gakkei". During Dr. Usui's lifetime the local Reiki center in Shizuoka, was headed by a Mr. Kozo Ogawa. Mr. Ogawa used to sell school uniforms and traveled from one school to another in the Shizuoka prefecture. Whenever he met with a sick child, he would treat it with Reiki. He was one of those rare healers who, like my wife Chetna, always knows how many sessions it will take to heal a certain disease. Mr. Oishi, for example, needed ten sessions for his eyesight problems. There was no noticeable change during the treatment, but after it was over, Mr. Oishi suddenly realized that his problems had subsided.

Dr. Usui recognized Mr. Ogawa's healing talents and ultimately elevated him to the highest rank in the organization. Dr. Usui and Mr. Ogawa used to give energy-charged crystal balls to their Reiki students. These crystal balls were placed directly on the patient's diseased area, helping the body to find its equilibrium again. After initiation, all students also received a manual that explained what Reiki is, described symptoms and gave guidelines for the treatment of illnesses.

People attending a Reiki meeting would kneel in traditional Japanese style, fold their hands in front of their chest

---

*The Japanese word *satori* cannot be translated as "enlightenment." *Sator* traditionally means a fleeting glimpse of a higher order or sudden understanding .

in the "gasho" or "namaste" position. The Reiki teacher would then touch the student's clasped hands with one hand and estimate their healing talent and energy. Mr. Oishi was told that his healing abilities were outstanding. Mr. Oishi attended Mr. Ogawa's Reiki meetings several times at quite a young age. At the beginning of each meeting, Mr. Ogawa would recite the five Reiki principles out loud.

He would also say that Dr. Usui spoke respectfully of the Meiji Emperor.

Mr. Ogawa ultimately opened a Reiki clinic in Shizuoka City where he gave Reiki treatment and initiated students. He had no children, and when he got too old to run the clinic, he asked Mr. Oishi to take over. Mr. Oishi declined after hearing that healing others would diminish his own life energy.

The adopted son of Mr. Ogawa, Mr. Fumio Ogawa, who took care of him in his old age, is still alive and spoke with Ms. Akimoto.

Dr. Usui founded the Usui Reiki Ryoho Gakkai (Usui Reiki Healing Method Society) with its seat in Tokyo and acted as its first president. There have been six presidents since, Mr. Ushida, Mr. Taketomi, Mr. Watanabe, Mr. Wanami, Mrs. Koyama, who retired in the beginning of 1998, and finally the present president of the Usui Reiki Ryoho Gakkai, Mr. Kondo. New members are accepted for a minimal membership fee.

By the time Mr. Ogawa learned Reiki in the 1940s, there were about 40 Reiki schools spread all over Japan. The system was divided into six degrees*, and made use of the same symbols we use today.

There is no evidence of additional symbols being used in Japan. The master symbol was not used extensively because the main focus of work was on healing and not on meditation. The absentee healing method was then called "the photograph method," and since not everyone could manage to have their photograph taken, it was mostly reserved for people who could afford it.

Conclusion

Having lived in Japan for many years now, I have always found it extremely unlikely that the presidency of the very traditional Usui Reiki Ryoho Gakkei should have been passed on to someone who was born and lived in a foreign country. According to our latest research, it appears that Mr. Hayashi was not in a position to choose the next president of the Reiki movement. Neither Mr. Oishi nor Mr. Ogawa recall the names of Mr. Hayashi, Ms. Takata, or any of the others who followed. It seems that somewhere along the line, East and West went their own separate ways. The world of Reiki is in a turmoil today. One school doesn't accept the other school as genuine or original, and the situation between the various Reiki teachers in North America and Europe borders on war. As if Reiki could ever belong to a country, a school, a concept, or even an individual!

I find myself in between the two worlds, in search of the essence. As far as I am concerned, everything is ONE. I believe that at this moment in time and space an ego-centered, sectarian way of thinking will only lead to disaster. We might destroy all that is beautiful in life, including Reiki, with our narrow-mindedness. The ego striving to be bigger and better than the next one will always try to differentiate. To remind us all of the one-ness of the universe with all its flowers and thorns, I would like to quote the beginning of the Isha Upanishad:

Aum—this is the whole.
That is the whole.
From wholeness emerges wholeness.
Wholeness coming from wholeness,
wholeness still remains.

Dr. Usui's Memorial Inscription

– In the memory of Usui Sensei's virtue –

Shortly after Dr. Usui's death, the Japanese Usui Shiki Ryoho built the afore-mentioned memorial for him at Saihoji temple in the Toyotama district of Tokyo. All in all, it took us a year to find the tomb. I flew to Tokyo to pay my respects. The Saihoji temple gave us the following directions: "Get off at Shinkoenji station, take a left and walk to the next traffic light. There you will find a police station, but don't ask the police because they don't know how to find us. Go across the street to the liquor store for directions instead." I was in the best of moods, since this sounded like true Zen! I was accompanied by two friends and fellow Reiki teachers. We did ask at the police station just for a lark, and, sure enough, they did send us the wrong way.

It was September 20th, 1994, the sky was overcast. The monk on duty told us where to find the grave and we took along some incense and a pail of water for a purification ritual. After we had burned the incense and cleaned the grave stone, I sat down to meditate. As soon as I used the Reiki Master symbol, the sun burst through the clouds with full force, filling me with light. The exact same thing happened to my wife when she paid her first visit to Dr. Usui's grave a year later.

The inscription on the Usui Memorial, written in old Japanese by Juzaburo Ushida and Masayuki Okada in February 1927, was translated into contemporary Japanese by Masano Kobayashi, my wife's mother. My wife and I did the translation from Japanese into English.*

"Someone who studies hard *(i.e. practices meditation)* and works assiduously to improve body and mind for the sake of becoming a better person is called "a man of great spirit." People who use that great spirit for a social purpose, that is, to teach the right way to many people and do collective good, are called "teachers." Dr. Usui was one such teacher.

---

*(...) comments by author and translator

He taught the Reiki of the universe *(universal energy)*. Countless people came to him and asked him to teach them the great way of Reiki and to heal them.

Dr. Usui was born in the first year of the Keio period, called Keio Gunnen, on August 15th (1864). His first name was Mikao and his other name is pronounced either Gyoho *(or Kyoho)*.* He was born in the village of Yago in the Yamagata district of Gifu prefecture. His ancestor's name is Tsunetane Chiba. His father's name was Uzaemon. His mother's family name was Kawaai. From what is known, he was a talented and hard-working student. As an adult he traveled to several Western countries and China to study, worked arduously, but did at point run into some bad luck. However he didn't give up and trained himself arduously.

One day he went to Mount Kurama on a 21-day retreat to fast and meditate. At the end of this period he suddenly felt the great Reiki energy at the top of his head, which led to the Reiki healing system. He first used Reiki on himself, then tried it on his family. Since it worked well for various ailments, he decided to share this knowledge with the public at large. He opened a clinic in Harajuku, Aoyama— Tokyo—in April of the 10th year of the Taisho period *(in 1921)*. He not only gave treatment to countless patients, some of whom had come from far and wide, but he also hosted workshops to spread his knowledge. In September of the twelfth year of the Taisho period *(1923)*, the devastating Kanto earthquake shook Tokyo. Thousands were killed, injured, or became sick in its aftermath. Dr. Usui grieved for his people, but he also took Reiki to the devastated city and used its healing powers on the surviving victims. His clinic soon became too small to handle the throng of patients, so in February of the 14th year of the Taisho period *(1925)*, he built a new one outside Tokyo in Nakano.

His fame spread quickly all over Japan, and invitations to distant towns and villages started coming in. Once he went to Kure, another time to Hiroshima prefecture, then to Saga prefecture and Fukuyama.

---

*It was an ancient Japanese custom for a teacher to give a new name to his student in order to break the continuity with the past and start anew. Sometimes a new name was adopted by the student himself.

It was during his stay in Fukuyama that he was hit by a fatal stroke on March 9th, of the fifteenth year of the Taisho period *(1926)*. He was 62 years of age.

Dr. Usui had a wife named Sadako; her maiden name was Suzuki. They had a son and a daughter. The son, Fuji Usui took over the family business after Dr. Usui's passing.

Dr. Usui was a very warm, simple and humble person. He was physically healthy and well-proportioned. He never showed off and always had a smile on his face; he was also very courageous in the face of adversity. He was, at the same time, a very cautious person. His talents were many. He liked to read, and his knowledge of medicine, psychology, fortune-telling and theology of religions around the world was vast. This life-long habit of studying and gathering information certainly helped pave the way to perceiving and understanding Reiki. *(I think this refers to his experience on Mount Kurama)*. Reiki not only heals diseases, but also amplifies innate abilities, balances the spirit, makes the body healthy, and thus helps achieve happiness. To teach this to others you should follow the five principles of the Meiji Emperor and contemplate them in your heart.

They should be spoken daily, once in the morning and once in the evening.

1) Don't get angry today.
2) Don't worry today.
3) Be grateful today.
4) Work hard today (meditative practice).
5) Be kind to others today.

The ultimate goal is to understand the ancient secret method for gaining happiness *(Reiki)* and thereby discover an all-purpose cure for many ailments. If these principles are followed you will achieve the great tranquil mind of the ancient sages. To begin spreading the Reiki system, it is important to start from a place close to you *(yourself)*, don't start from something distant such as philosophy or logic.

Sit still and in silence every morning and every evening with your hands folded in the "Ghasso" or "Namaste". Follow the great principles, and be clean and quiet. Work on your heart and do things from the quiet space inside of you. Anyone can access Reiki, because it begins within yourself!

Philosophical paradigms are changing the world round. If Reiki can be spread throughout the world it will touch the human heart and the morals of society. It will be helpful for many people, and will not only heal disease, but also the Earth as a whole. Over 2000 people learned Reiki from Dr. Usui. More learned it from his senior disciples, and they carried Reiki even further. Even now after Dr. Usui's passing, Reiki will spread far and wide for a long time to come. It is a universal blessing to have received Reiki from Dr. Usui and to be able to pass it on to others. Many of Dr. Usui's students converged to build this memorial here at Saihoji Temple in the Toyotoma district.

I was asked to write these words to help keep his great work alive. I deeply appreciate his work and I would like to say to all of his disciples that I am honored to have been chosen for this task. May many understand what a great service Dr. Usui did to the world."

My Reiki Adventure

I learned Reiki in Berlin, Germany, in late 1992. The aim was to deepen my understanding of the body-mind system and for my own pleasure.

At this point, I would like to thank my teacher from the bottom of my heart for all the love and care he put into teaching me Reiki. For reasons I don't understand, he doesn't want his name mentioned in this book.

I was not interested in teaching Reiki and honestly speaking I wanted to stay as far away as possible from the so called "New Age" movement. As soon as I got back to Japan, I initiated my wife Chetna M. Kobayashi and got the first taste of teaching Reiki. I realized that I loved the initiations themselves, which put both teacher and student in a wonderful state of oneness.

Chetna then initiated her mother into the First Degree and had a similar experience to the one I had when I initiated

31

her, we decided to share the Third and Teacher's Degree with all interested people in Japan.

The response to our first advertisements in the "Tama" and "Osho Times" magazines was quite overwhelming. Reiki One and Two had been taught by several teachers in Japan for many years, but this was the first time that Reiki Three and the Teacher's Degree workshops were made available to everyone. Many people who had been initiated into one or two degrees came to us (and are still coming) from all over Japan.

Before starting to teach the Teachers Degree, we decided to give future Reiki teachers all the know how necessary to perform initiations themselves, in order to spread Reiki more quickly. By now, many of our students and their students are teaching Reiki in Japan, it is spreading like wild fire. I would like to thank everyone who shared their life with us in the past. I'm looking forward to sharing myself and Reiki as long as there is a need for it.

May all beings be happy.

The Five Reiki Principles

The five principles originally laid down as guidelines for a fulfilled life by the Meiji Emperor of Japan (1868-1912) were adopted up by Dr. Usui to incorporate into our lives, and help us be a channel for the universal life energy. I do not believe that these are mere moral codes meant to be followed doggedly.

Suppression of one's thoughts and emotions can never be of any help the person seeking enlightenment. These guidelines are simply stepping stones on the path towards increased awareness of the macro- and microcosmos. The red thread running through each of these guidelines is oneness of the individual and the cosmos.

1) Don't get angry today.
There is nothing inherently wrong with anger. It is just a sign that you are trying to swim against the natural current

of events. When anger knocks at your door, the most sensible way to deal with it is to acknowledge it, observe it and, in so doing, let it go forever. Once you cease identifying with the emotion, the fire dies down. A very effective method of dealing with anger and other forms of (seemingly uncontrollable) access energies before they occur is Dynamic Meditation*, which is being used by countless Western psychologists and psychotherapists for stress relief and emotional release. By means of controlled catharsis, we can rid ourselves of undesirable tensions.

2) Don't worry today.
We worry to keep ourselves separate from the whole, to attain a sensation of being special that we are unable to feel otherwise. We worry that things might turn out differently from what we expected, and consider only our own advantage. The source of worry is fear of that one thing we can ever be absolutely sure of: change.

We tend to see the rest of humanity as competitors and maybe even foes instead of fellow travelers. We forget that the universe is one, and only the ego tears it to pieces.

3) Be grateful today.
We all know how hard it is to look at every experience with new eyes each time. And yet, when we perchance do, the moment seems eternal and magical. In consciously appreciating our surroundings, be that our partner or the tiniest blade of grass, we can once again find our own place in this tremendously beautiful tale of life.

So-called "good and bad" are a part of everything in life. I remember an ancient tale told to me by my master Osho Rajneesh:

In a little village out in the country, there lived an old man, who owned a very beautiful horse. Even though he was very poor he always turned down offers to buy his horse because it had become like a friend to him. The other villagers thought him eccentric and stupid because he could have ended his

*The Orange Book by Osho Rajneesh

poverty by selling the horse. One day, the horse's stable was found to be empty. The villagers were convinced that the animal had been stolen and agreed that the old man would have been better off selling it in the first place. The old man remarked that the only ascertainable fact was that the horse was absent from the stable and told the others not to judge the situation. A while later, the horse came back by itself bringing with him a dozen wild horses. Now the villagers thought that a great fortune had come to the old man, but again he told them only to look at the facts and not to judge a small fragment of reality without knowing the whole.

The old man's only son soon started to train the wild horses. One day he fell and broke his legs. The villagers again thought that this was a great calamity since he was the only help his father had. But the old man stuck to his non-judgmental viewpoint. Soon after a war broke out with a neighboring kingdom and all the young men of the state were drafted except the old man's crippled son ... The story goes on forever.

We tend to look at our own and others' lives from a very narrow perspective, not knowing the whole, not trusting and not rejoicing in the moment, whatever it offers us. Let's give it a try!

4) Work hard today (meditative practice)

This principle does not suggest you do some job 12 hours a day. The term "hard work" refers to work on ourselves, practicing meditation and devoting our time to spiritual growth. Inner world values differ considerably from those of the outer world. "Working hard" on the outside turns into "devotion" on the inside, where hardness has no place. In the outside world we may be working towards a goal, yet in the inner world the actual moment is the only time there is. Practicing awareness or meditation in daily activities is the purpose of many Eastern religions and was introduced to the West by the famous Armenian mystic G.I. Gurdijeff, who called it self-remembrance. Reiki, in my mind, aims at attaining the same state of mind. Meditation cannot be forced, but the stone must be thrown into the pond first before ripples move to each and every shore. After all these years, meditation has become subtle but essential nourishment to me, the best food I have had up to now in fact! You will find more on meditation in chapter "Meditation."

5) Be kind to others today.
All hierarchies are man-made. What they cause is there for all to see: environmental destruction, global warming, never-ending wars and so on; the list is heartbreaking and endless. Look at the environment with a loving heart, and the world once again turns into a miraculous space that feeds on love.

Of course, this guideline is also meant to be understood internally, within oneself. Friendliness to all beings must include yourself. In fact you should be the platform from which to start your loving journey. Sages throughout the ages have been known to "worship" their own bodies to the bewilderment of the people around. Yet seen in this light, it doesn't seem strange at all.

Practical Part

The Reiki Degrees

The Reiki system, according to the legacy of Dr. Usui, consists of three or four degrees depending on the school. The difference lies only in how the degrees are divided up. The Second and Third Degree symbols are almost identical. The slight variations in the symbols stem from the fact that they were given to students on different levels on the path. Some Reiki schools claim to teach the "original teaching" and put down all the others. The truth is that there is no original teaching! Reiki is alive and therefore always changing, always flowing and expanding. Reiki and dogmatism don't mix.

In the following chapter I will give a general description of each degree and its function the way we teach it. A detailed description of the Second and Third Degree symbols cannot be given in a book. It can only be passed on to the student by a teacher. It would be of no help to anyone not (yet) initiated into Second or Third Degree Reiki. The initiation methods will not be mentioned at all. It is a well-guarded secret passed on only to those who want to share Reiki, which means sharing themselves with others.

The First Degree

The First Degree is meant to reconnect us with our own physical form, the thing so close to ourselves and yet so distant. Normally we only feel our own body when we are in pain or discomfort. The physical body is the crudest extension of our soul, a miraculous vehicle that enables us to move about and feel and understand endless situations in daily life. It helps us experience (and eventually understand) pain and pleasure, bliss and agony. Getting in touch with our own bodies again also helps us tune into someone else's body and, by extension, their being.

Usually, the first Reiki Degree consists of four initiations and workshops, which can be held on either one or two days, depending on the school and the size of the group. Some schools, especially Reiki teachers who initiate large groups at once, initiate the First Degree only once or twice. The initiation process differs a little from school to school, but I have tried out several methods and found that they all work.

Before the first initiation students are taught what Reiki is, its objectives and origins.

After this introduction, they receive their first initiation. They are shown photographs of the twelve hand positions that are used to transfer energy from practitioner to the receiver. (You will find drawings of the twelve main positions and several auxiliary ones both for use on yourself and others in the hands-on section of this book.)

They are initiated again a few minutes later. After this second initiation, they try out the positions they have just learned on themselves for an hour. Even after the first initiation, the feeling of energy flowing through your hands is surprisingly strong and quite incontrovertible. Reiki doesn't require you to believe in it at all.

With each following initiation the energy gets stronger and stronger. People who are able to see auras have been known to detect a very clear difference in the aura of a Reiki student before and after the first and subsequent initiations. Each initiation takes about 10-15 minutes (per person).

After the third initiation the group participants pair up and exchange a full session with each another.

It is important to always keep your fingers together when using the Reiki hand positions. It is not necessary for your hands to get hot in each position, and you will find that different parts of the body draw more energy and others less. No Reiki session is ever the same, since every individual is unique and in constant change. I am reminded of the ancient saying by Heraclitus "You can't step into the same river twice."

Then comes the fourth initiation.

At the end of the workshop the participants are given the First Reiki Degree certificate and are asked to go through a period of purification for the next 21 days. That means giving yourself a full Reiki session daily, drinking lots of water or herbal teas, and refraining from heavy drinking and other drugs. This is not a moral issue, but rather a means to intensify and deepen the First Degree initiations.

Reiki energy is very subtle. It usually takes some time for a beginner to tune into it and appreciate it fully. With each initiation, the chakras are tuned to a higher frequency, which brings about the following (provided you are open to it):

- *Magnification of our inner perception.* We develop greater sensitivity for the energy of others, of things and, of course, of ourselves. This also involves sharpening our intuition, a sense that has been neglected for too long.
- *Growing self-confidence and trust in life as a benevolent force.* When we find out that we are just a tiny part of this orchestra, we realize that existence wants the best for all of its parts and we can stop resisting it for a change. Let go!
- *More compassion towards everyone and everything, including ourselves.* By focusing on the universal life energy from now on, we become aware of the fact that separation is an illusion. We all live on the same fuel.
- *Growing responsibility for our own life and being.* We will start to take our life into our own hands and work together with existence instead against it.
- *Solving old problems.* One of the side effects of a Reiki initiation is that many unsolved problems reportedly bubble up in order to be resolved. Of course it is up to us to answer the call. Reiki is not a magic pill that takes care of our ailments while we go about business as usual. Personal growth and change require determination!

As a rule, I would suggest you not offer Reiki sessions too freely and not without some kind of compensation, which does not have to be money. It is very difficult to take in, accept and appreciate something given for "free." Of course, within your own family and between close friends the rules are different, since a constant exchange of energy is always taking place anyway.

First Degree Reiki can also be applied to pets, other animals, plants, crystals, electronics, in short everything sentient and insentient. The hand positions for animals remain the same since animal organs are located in the same place as humans. If the animal is very small, the best place to touch or hold it would be right behind the ears. The length of the "session" obviously depends on the animal itself! It will just take off when it has had enough. Dogs usually enjoy Reiki, and I have heard both negative and positive reports about cats. Our cat just loves it.

Fish can be treated by touching the walls of the aquarium and thereby charging the water.

Potted plants and trees take in a large percentage of their nutrition through the roots, so the most efficient way to treat them is to embrace the pot with both of your hands and let the energy flow. The same can be done with the watering can before feeding, fertilizing, or spraying your plants.

Trees can be energized by embracing the trunk with your whole body. All sorts of flora responds very well to Reiki treatment.*

Food and drinks can be energized if they taste bad or you aren't sure whether or not they were prepared with love. It is probably a good idea to do this whenever you eat in big commercial restaurants.

Medicine can be held in your hand for a while before taking it. Crystals can be easily charged with Reiki energy just by letting the energy flow while holding them.

Things in general can be given energy to prolong their life or intensify their performance by either laying your hands on them or holding them in your hands, depending on their size. The same goes for photographs of people or places.

A very effective way to energize something regularly is the so-called Reiki box. To make your own, take any suitable box, big enough to stuff with one or, even better, several pieces of paper or photographs.

Choose carefully whatever it is you wish to energize. Question each one of them, and when you have decided what to work on, simply close the box and hold it in your hands every day for at least a week. Let the energy flow.

More efficient methods will be discussed in the Second Degree chapter.

---

*Peter Tompkins, Christopher Bird, *The Secret Life Of Plants*, Harper & Row, ISBN 0-06-091587-0

First, however, I would like to describe a few exercises that will help you probe your inner world and experience your body more profoundly as part of yourself.

- Touch yourself as if you were touching your beloved. From early childhood on, we have been taught not to touch ourselves lovingly. As a result, we always associate a loving touch with sex and sex alone. Fall in love with your own body, and it will let you know what is and isn't helpful for your health.
- Choose your nutrition conscientiously. Our diet tends to be haphazard (i.e., depending on availability) or determined by an outside agency/system (diet plan, society, education). We never inquire, never ask our own body what it needs for its nourishment. If you like to work with a pendulum you can use it to work out your menu. Another way of tuning into your own body is to meditate before meals. When you are in a state of silence and vulnerability ask your body what it would like to eat.
- Feel your body from the inside. This is an ancient Indian meditation technique, devised by the god Shiva, that lets you enter your body—your foot, for example—and feel it from within. We always experience our body from the outside only. What does the inside of your foot look like, what colors do you see, what do muscles, nerves and arteries look like? Become intimately familiar with your body.
- A similar method is to reduce your consciousness to a tiny point and let it move through your physical form from toes to head.
- When using the Reiki hand positions on yourself, breathe into each one as you go along.
- A Taoist grounding exercise: Stand in a relaxed position for three to five minutes, legs spread to shoulder width. Hold your arms stretched out at the side of your body at shoulder level. Your left palm should face upwards, your right palm downwards.
- Review your day before going to sleep. It is important to go backwards, from night to morning. This exercise prevents your day's undigested experiences from invad-

ing your night. When practiced regularly, you can use this method to go back into your childhood and even further ...

* Keep a Reiki Journal. Write a few lines daily or weekly describing how Reiki is affecting and changing your life.

The Second Degree

Second Degree Reiki takes us further into ourselves and gives us more powerful tools for self-discovery and integration. With the help of several symbols we learn to let the universal life energy flow more efficiently. The Second and Third Degree Reiki symbols should be kept absolutely secret. Some schools even go so far as to forbid students to write them down. I believe it is all right to write them down, but they should be kept away from uninitiated eyes.

Second Degree Reiki can be used in the same situations as First Degree, except that now we can use either symbol to intensify the effect. With these symbols we learn to make direct contact with our subconscious/superconscious mind: The Second Degree can help us heal not only our own (or someone else's) body, but emotions and mind as well. Healing the physical body can bring about momentary relief from discomfort, but in the long run it is important to balance the whole being.

The Second Degree initiations work on a higher level than the First Degree initiations, mainly on the etheric body. We are also taught a method of absentee healing across time and space. This may sound incredible at first, but it really isn't as outlandish as it seems. Thoughts, emotions and energy travel just like electromagnetic waves from one point in space to another. The Second Degree Reiki initiation turns us into energy-transmitters across time and space!

Workshops, initiations and even the symbols vary slightly from school to school.

Some schools don't give the name (or mantra) of the symbols to their students, while others do. Some schools initiate the Second Reiki Degree in one initiation, but we do it in three. This does not mean that "our" Reiki is better than "their" Reiki, only the process is different. Second Degree workshops usually take a full day, and many schools combine it with the First Degree.

I personally think it best (in most cases) to let a few weeks elapse between First, Second and Third Degree initiations, in order to allow for some time to understand the material, the word "understand" being in the fundamental, not intellectual, sense. My experience shows that it takes at least three months to grasp the profoundness of the Second Reiki Degree with all its variations...

We always begin our workshops by getting to know each other and then reviewing the last degree. There are usually many unanswered questions, and it takes a few hours just to get ready for the first initiation. After the first initiation, students are shown the first symbol and taught how and when to use it. Those of you who are not initiated into Second Degree Reiki can skip this part of the book because it cannot be understood before having attended a Second Degree Reiki workshop.

Students are then shown the following grounding exercise and are asked to practice their new skill:
Imagine the power symbol in both of your foot chakras (in the arch of your feet). When you feel it there, imagine it in your hara (two inches below your navel). As soon as you can feel it in your hara, imagine it in both of your hand chakras (in the center of the palm of your hands).

This exercise puts us back into our center and can be used before giving sessions or when one feels uncomfortable or "airy." It can also help before meditation. The power symbol can be used to energize drinking water or foods, medicines and even machines. It can be used as protection by placing it in front of, next to and behind yourself, or to clear a room or house by setting it into each corner. This symbol also stops physical pain.

In the second initiation, the students are shown the mental healing symbol and are taught when and how to use it. Again there are some exercises to learn and practice:

Just like in the First Degree workshop, students now perform hands-on sessions on each other using the two symbols they have learned. The symbols magnify the transferred energy and halve the time spent on each position.

The first two symbols can be used to charge crystals as well.

There is a deprogramming technique that helps us dissolve agonizing behavior patterns. Formulate an affirmation and proceed as follows:

Draw the power symbol on the back of your head and hold your hands there. Now draw the mental healing symbol on the medulla (where the spine begins) and use the power symbol again. Put one hand on your forehead and one on your medulla. Imagine that you are being flooded with light from head to toe. Say the affirmation in your mind three times. Practice this technique on yourself or others on six consecutive days and then twice a week.

A nice way to help us relax whenever we take a bath is to send the first two symbols into the tub before getting in.

After the third initiation, students are shown the absentee healing symbol and how to use it. They are asked to do the following exercise: Use the absentee healing symbol and put it on the third eye of the receiver, then let it be followed by the power symbol. Say the person's name three times in your mind and then proceed with the healing. You can either imagine the receiver lying in front of you or imagine the receiver being enveloped in your clasped hands, whatever suits you best. In general absentee healings should not exceed 15 minutes.

The following method helps with karma resolution:

Lay the absentee healing symbol on the situation, person, place in your unresolved past. Then send the mental healing symbol and afterwards the power symbol. Ask for forgiveness or forgive.

The third symbol can also be used during meditation. It can help connect us with a person, an enlightened one, a place, a certain time, in short we can connect with anything in and beyond space and time.

Before meditating, I often use the absentee healing symbol and then repeat in my mind three times *"Here and now, here and now, here and now."* Then I let the power symbol follow. With this method you can manage to discourage intrusive daydreams ...

I have heard that the absentee healing method should not be used during operations because the symbols could affect the anesthetic.

However, I always use it on myself when I sitting in the dentist's chair, and I enjoy my dental treatments immensely! By using the symbols, you can create (or just see?) a gap between your body and the pain, as if the pain were happening to someone else!

I also use the symbols to help me drive to work and back safely. First I use the absentee healing symbol, repeating in my mind *"safety, safety, safety,"* then I send the mental healing symbol to the space between the road and my front and rear bumpers, and finally the power symbol. Second Degree Reiki can also help the dying make their transition in a positive, relaxed and conscious way.

Exercises:
- Place either symbol in your chakras and feel it there. You will find that a symbol may feel good in one chakra and not good in another.
- Do the same with your organs or whole body parts.
- Visualize either symbol with your inner eye and look at it for several minutes. If this is difficult and you would like to train your visualization powers, do the following: Cut a piece of cardboard approximately 30 cm by 30 cm. Glue a piece of black paper of the same size onto it. Then draw one of the symbols on a piece of white paper and cut it out so you end up with a white symbol 15 cm by 15 cm in size. Glue it to the center of the black surface and attach the whole drawing to a white wall. Stand or sit 3 feet away, close your eyes and relax. Imagine yourself to be surrounded by warm and soothing darkness for a few minutes. Now open your eyes and look at the center of the pattern for two minutes without straining them. Focus softly. Don't stare but try not to blink your eyes either. After two minutes, turn away from the pattern and look at the white wall. You will see the image "printed" on your retina, a white square and a black symbol. When it fades away, try to recreate it and then close your eyes and imagine the

symbol in front of your inner eye. This exercise done for a few weeks will strengthen your powers of visualization and memory immensely!

- Energize the whole day in the morning using the absentee healing symbol, the mental healing symbol, and then the power symbol.
- Make a Reiki box as described above and proceed as follows:
  Use the absentee healing symbol to bring an issue into focus. Repeat the issue or the name of the person three times in your mind. Use the mental healing symbol and finally the power symbol.
- Write the power symbol or the mental healing symbol (or both) on a piece of cloth and put it under your mattress or pillow.

The Third Degree (3a)

In the Third Degree workshop, the student is initiated into the Reiki Master symbol. There is little to be said about the Third Reiki Degree, except that the Master symbol consciously connects us to the divine spark. Some people call it the "higher self." I don't particularly like that expression, because it is easily misunderstood to mean that there is something like a higher, bigger, or better ego that talks to us. What I call the divine spark is beyond all words and language. It is pure "being," the center of existence, that can be found only in absolute silence, within and without.

Third Degree Reiki is mainly used for private meditation. After the Third Degree, the Reiki system is basically complete. The Master symbol can be used at any time and as often as you wish to "reinitiate" yourself, if you will.

A helpful exercise is to use Third Degree Reiki just before falling asleep, often you will find yourself carrying its fragrance through the night and waking up consciously in the morning.

The Fourth Degree (3b)

In the Fourth Degree, students are taught how to initiate others into all of the above degrees (some Reiki schools and individual teachers teach only how to initiate the first two degrees).

The Fourth Degree is only of interest to people who want to share Reiki—and therefore themselves—with others.

Personally, I love to initiate others into Reiki because it gives me the chance to meet my fellow travelers on a very deep and loving level, beyond judgment, preferences and aversions. Since the teacher is just a channel for Reiki energy, initiations pour through him or her just as they pour through the student. This process creates a wonderful sense of oneness.

However, working as a Reiki teacher is not everyone's calling and requires more than just the initiation process know how. Actually one should be a skilled communicator, counselor and lover of humanity before setting out to teach a thing as delicate as Reiki. Above all, I feel the Reiki teacher should keep in mind that the relationship to his or her student is mutual and both should be filled with a sense of gratitude. Without the teacher a student can't learn, but without a student a teacher can't teach!

Teaching Reiki is very rewarding most of the time, but there is a darker side to it as well. During the Teacher's Degree and often thereafter, the former student's attitude can change. As my wife Chetna recently told me: "You really find out who your friends are during the Teacher's Degree training."

Some people are so attached to the idea of duality, of me and you, that they can't stand the idea of having learned Reiki (or anything for that matter) from someone else.

Anyone who teaches in the so-called spiritual world is bound to encounter this problem sooner or later. Some people will downright hate you for having taught them!

However, there is a lesson to be learned here, a lesson in unconditional trust, something that all of us will eventually have to learn.

To close this chapter I would like to quote a Zen story my master Osho told me on June 20th, 1988, the so-called **quantum leap from mind to no-mind (#10):**

Nansen was living in a little hut in the mountains. One day, a strange monk visited him just as he was preparing to go to his work in the fields. Nansen welcomed him saying: "Please make yourself at home. Cook anything you like for your lunch, then bring some of the leftover food to me along the road leading to my work place."

Nansen worked hard until evening and came home very hungry. The stranger had cooked and enjoyed a good meal all by himself, then had thrown away all the provisions and broken all the utensils. Nansen found the monk sleeping peacefully in the empty hut, but when he stretched his own tired body beside the stranger's, the latter got up and went away. Years later, Nansen told the anecdote to his disciples with the comment: "He was such a good monk, I miss him even now."

The Reiki Session

In a Reiki session, the hands are laid on the "receiver" using twelve or more hand positions that correspond to the major chakras or energy centers in our body.* When administering Reiki, your fingers should touch each other. This balances the energy flowing from your hands. You should spend about five minutes on each position. From the hand position the energy finds its own way to where it is needed most and floods both the "giver" and "receiver" with relaxation and a sense of well-being. If the receiver cannot be touched directly, the hands can be held 3-5 cm above the specific position with the same effect. The receiver is usually fully dressed and should either be lying down or sitting. Arms and legs shouldn't be crossed so as not to hinder the flow of energy. A full session takes about one hour, but it can be condensed in case of emergency. Also, certain body parts can be treated separately. No effort is involved on your part in a Reiki session. In fact the less you involve yourself, the better. Reiki doesn't involve drawing out or dissolving "bad" energy, it just helps the universal life energy to flow again.

Use a well-aired and well-lighted room that is clean and comfortable for both the giver and the receiver. The room temperature should be around 21-23°C, and a blanket should be kept handy. Many people feel cold when they relax.

The best ways to perform a Reiki session is on a massage table, but a bed, chair, or even a thick carpet or several pillows will do the job too. To create a hallowed environment for the session many practitioners use soft lighting or even candles. Some people decorate their session room with pictures or statues of enlightened beings or with other soul-soothing articles. Some like to play soft classical or New Age music at low volume while treating their clients. Others burn incense or use any number of other means to clear the energy of a room before giving a session. This is entirely up to the individual's style and intuition.

---

*There are minor chakras as well for instance in the palms of both hands.

The colors of your interior decor and the clothes you wear also influence the atmosphere in your session room and hence the outcome of the Reiki session. To encourage an atmosphere of love, the color pink is helpful. For healing use green, for calmness blue, and for energy release red. To encourage a clear intellect yellow and for a peaceful state of mind, use black.

For the practitioner it is helpful to find a quiet space detached from personal affairs before touching a client, but it is not a must for "success." Personally, I find it very helpful to remember that we are touching the divine every time we give a session or an initiation to a fellow being. Feel grateful to the person for allowing you to touch her or him. The key to a delightful Reiki session for the practitioner is the right attitude. Since Reiki energy is not yours and you are just acting as a channel for it, your moods don't influence the outcome of a session for another person. Prior to a session, both giver and receiver should wash their hands and take off all metal accessories, belts, and the like. Metal may influence the natural flow of energy.

The receiver should be told beforehand about what a session involves so that there can be silence during the session, except for gentle commands like "please turn over," etc.

What happens next is hard to explain since it varies from one person to the other. Most people, like myself, feel as if they were back in their mother's womb while on the receiving end of a Reiki session. We are enveloped by a feeling of carefree well-being, all worries dissolve into thin air, and we may even forget where we are. For me, it often resembles a combination of deep sleep and awareness. Afterwards, I feel refreshed and grateful to the giver and all that surrounds us. We feel in tune with existence again.

Sessions should be given on four consecutive days and, if treatment is to be extended, it is good to repeat them twice a week for a time period of your choice.

Following is a list of what we have found to be suitable music for Reiki sessions:

- Any Reiki music that you personally like, such as W.M. Zapp O. Ilios Healing Music for Reiki, Merlin's Magic, Ajad Reiki Music Vol. 1-3, Anuvida Healing Hands, etc.

- Brian Eno, Music For Airports, Neroli, The Pearl
- Deuter, Celebration, Ecstasy and others
- Classical European music
- Kitaro, Silk Road, etc.
- Georgia Kelly, Seapeace
- Environmental music
- Most New Age music, if it is uplifting.

Benefits

Reiki has helped me find more balance between body, mind and spirit. I have fallen in love with my body again, after 30 years of treating it like a lifeless tool. I have become more sensitive to the energy of situations, both positive and negative, and have found the courage to appreciate them all. Reiki has also helped in my meditating, making it easier for me to probe into my inner depths. I use the Second and Third Degree symbols with pleasure for my daily meditations. My overall health has become more balanced and life is more fun than ever before. I have also learned to allow myself to be sick, to give my body the space, time and attention it needs to recuperate without judgment and anxiety. Another dramatic change is that my wife and I have become much more sensitive to the energy of people, things and places. It has become almost impossible for me to eat food prepared without love, to read books that weren't written by a loving heart and to listen to music that is born out of confusion. My compassion has grown, and I often find myself cool and collected in situations that used to set me on fire in the past.

In general, we can say that Reiki fills our lives with joy and happiness. If we are ill, it gives us back the will to live. We have repeatedly experienced and heard this from people with "terminal illnesses." Reiki helps us see others more lovingly, it puts us into a gentle equilibrium of body, mind and soul and helps us act and be more responsible with our life.

To list all the benefits that a person may experience from a Reiki initiation would fill a whole library since each and every one of us is unique. Especially after Second and Third Degree initiations many of us go through dramatic changes in our personal lives, relationships or in our work. So if you are afraid of change it is best you stay away from Reiki!

Basic Head Positions

Position 1

Position 2

Position 3

Position 4

The Reiki Hand Positions and Their Functions

The original Reiki system as conceived by Dr. Usui did not include a system of hand positions as we now use them. He simply healed by relying on his intuition, letting his hands do the thinking. It is said that he used only one hand to heal while he held a ball of "energy" in the other (a practice widely followed in some Chinese Qigong healing styles).

The current system was developed later. After many years of experimenting it was found that Reiki energy flows more easily when the hands are held on or over the body in a certain sequence of hand positions. I have found very similar—sometimes identical—healing hand positions in systems from many different cultures. The following positions are the most commonly used. I have added a few extra ones at the end of the chapter.

The Basic Head Positions
1) Head #1 relaxes and dissolves stress and fear.
Good for sinus problems, eye, nose, tooth and jaw ailments. Balances pineal and pituitary glands, which correspond to the 6th and 7th chakras.

2) **Head #2** improves memory and synchronizes the left and right brain. Good for headaches and earaches, assists the dying.

3) **Head #3** relaxes, dissolves stress and calms the mind. Good for problems concerning the cerebellum and spinal marrow, as well as headaches.

4) **Head #4** builds self-confidence, and gives more joy and self- respect. Magnifies creativity. Good for throat, tonsil, and thyroid problems. Corresponds to the 5th chakra.

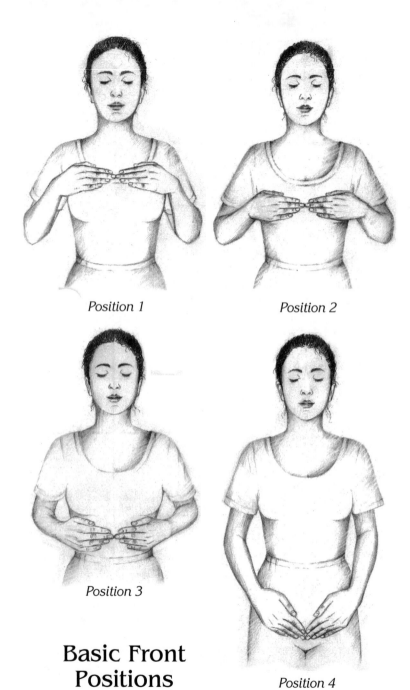

Position 1

Position 2

Position 3

Basic Front
Positions

Position 4

The Basic Front Positions

5) **Front #1** enhances love, trust and harmony. Affects the thymus gland, which corresponds to the heart chakra. Good for the lungs and cardiovascular system.

6) **Front #2** helps dispel fear and stress. Affects the solar plexus or 3rd chakra. Good for liver, stomach, gallbladder, spleen and digestive tract.

7) **Front #3** is similar to #2. This position dispels fear and stress. Affects the 2nd and 3rd chakras. Good for liver, stomach, gallbladder, spleen and digestive tract.

8) **Front #4** dispels sexual fears and tensions. Affects the 1st and 2nd chakras and is good for the ovaries and uterus in women, prostate in men, and the bladder and digestive tract in both.

The Basic Back Positions

The back positions are basically the same as the front positions.

9) **Back #1** helps against stress, and promotes relaxation. Good for spine and neck problems.

10) **Back #2** is the same as front #2.

11) **Back #3** is the same as front #3. Good for the kidneys.

12) **Back #4** is the same as front #4. Good for tailbone injuries.

The Extra Positions

1) One hand on the forehead, and the other on the back of the head. This position is also called the cosmic plug, because it helps 'recharge' our own or the recipient's energies.

2) One hand on the heart chakra and one hand on the hara. This position has been known to help with insomnia. It gives us a gentle feeling before beginning our night's sleep.

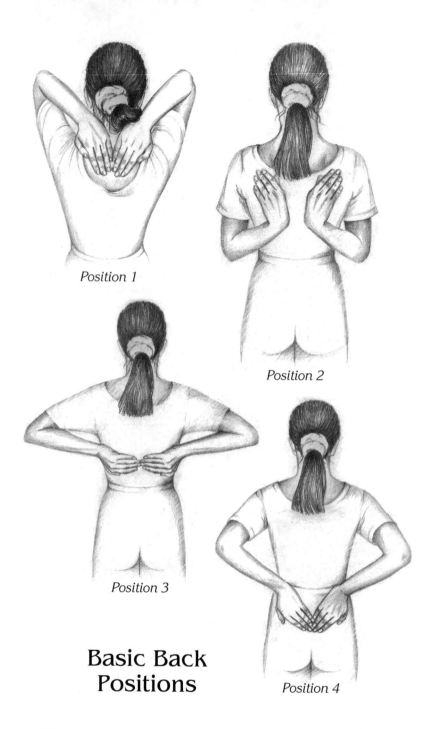

Position 1

Position 2

Position 3

Basic Back
Positions

Position 4

3) Both hands on the heart chakra. This position also helps us fall asleep.

4) One hand on the heart chakra and the other on the solar plexus. Has a similar effect as #1.

The Chakra Positions

Some Reiki schools, namely Osho Reiki or Neo Reiki, teach almost exclusively chakra positions instead of the more common basic positions. They are just as good as the ones mentioned above and if those are the ones you have learned, you should use them primarily to deepen your understanding.

For a quick Reiki session I sometimes use only the following eight positions:*
1) Both hands on the top of the head.
2) One hand on the forehead, one on the back of the head.
3) One hand on the throat, one behind it.
4) One hand on the heart chakra, one on the back of it.
5) One hand on the solar plexus, one on the back of it.
6) One hand on the hara, one on the back of it.
7) One hand on the first chakra, one on the back of it.
8) One hand on the sole of the right foot, one hand on the sole of the left foot.

---

*Here the hands can be held 5-10 cm (2-4 inches) above the body too.

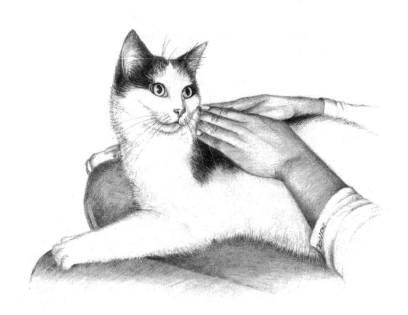

Cats love Reiki ...

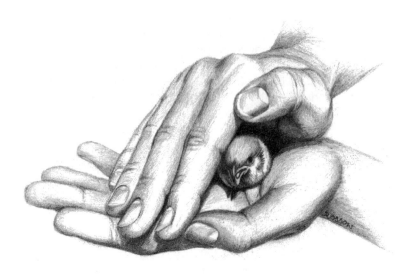

... and it´s also good for tiny birds

Reiki Stories

Reiki is not a miracle cure for all ailments. As a holistic healing method, it usually needs time to help the receiver's system rebalance itself. However, "instant healing" does occur occasionally as a result of an initiation or even a single hands-on session. Minor ailments like headaches or stomachaches, coughs, and muscular pains are often, though not always, balanced within minutes.

In the next chapter, I will share some of our Reiki experiences and those of our friends. Please keep in mind at all times, that these stories are individual ones: Healing depends on the entire physical, psychological and emotional history of each Reiki practitioner or patient. A healing of the same disease may or may not occur in two different people. In any case, healing can never be promised, we are only a tool in the hands of the universal life energy. Whatever happens, if it doesn't wish to happen, doesn't happen. Some diseases are karmic in nature and they may fail to heal even after the karmic objective has been achieved.

At any rate, here are the stories:

- My wife's mother, who had been suffering from insomnia for years due to stress, managed to quit her sleeping pills just a few days after receiving the First Reiki Degree. She has been treating herself daily ever since and has never had to take medication again. When going to sleep, it is helpful to place the hands on the extra position #1.

- My mother, who had been suffering from cataracts, received the First Degree Reiki from my brother last year and has improved considerably, she can see the stars again! She uses position #1 a great deal, which has also helped with a chronic sinus problem. When she recently had to spend a few days in hospital to have a little lump in her breast removed, the whole family sent her Reiki by the absentee method. She recovered from the anesthesia within minutes to the surprise of doctors and nurses and was able to go home after a few hours.

- One of our friends, Mr. I. from Tokyo, reported that since he received the last two Reiki degrees many of his small wishes have been fulfilled. The funny part of the story is, he said, that his wishes are fulfilled after he has forgotten about them!

- A friend of ours, Ms. H. from Osaka, who was here for a First Degree initiation, went through a catharsis right after the first initiation, it had brought up memories of an unresolved family tragedy, and by going through the pain again, the healing started. Her sister had been suffering from severe, debilitating premenstrual pains for the past seven years and could not move without the help of her relatives. Right after receiving the First Degree Reiki initiations, her monthly pains disappeared completely.

- Tao's operation. About a week after our cat was sterilized, she wanted nothing but Reiki. Every time we sat on the couch, she would jump on our laps and stay there for hours, soaking up the energy. Both my wife and I felt her belly to be like a black hole continuously drawing energy. As soon as she felt better, she stopped the treatments herself and went back to her regular routine of being an independent pet. The wounds healed rapidly leaving no scars. The same thing happens every time she gets into a fight with another cat and comes home all scratched up.

- My wife's cousin owns a dairy farm in northern Hokkaido. A newly-born calf was refusing to drink milk while we were visiting. The calf would buck when we tried to feed it, but after a few minutes of Reiki treatment (using the absentee method), it finally started to accept and enjoy its meals.

- My wife and I own and operate a language school in Sapporo, and we use Reiki on our computers when they seem to have functional problems. It may sound farfetched, but since everything is permeated by the universal life energy, even machines can react to Reiki positively. At one point we even discouraged a vicious computer virus from doing its damage.

- One thing I have personally experienced several times, and have also heard from friends, is that Reiki can diminish or even eliminate the effects of jet lag. Last time I flew from Japan to Germany and back, I felt as if I had just gone for a short walk. The time difference didn't seem to bother me at all: I felt fresh and energetic.

- *Accidents:* One day last summer, I tried to repair our garage door myself, instead of listening to my intuition, which said that I should leave it to a professional. But I do have a rather stubborn disposition ... I ended up being hit by a large spring-loaded gadget, which inflicted deep and painful cuts to my left hand and shoulder. I received first-aid Reiki from my wife, and after holding her hands over my swollen shoulder for about ten minutes, the swelling was completely gone and I could laugh about my stupidity. The greatest twist was that the cuts on my shoulder looked exactly like the Chinese hexagram for "enthusiasm!"
One Summer we went camping with 20 of our students. The camping area near Sapporo was infested with giant wasps. Two of the kids were stung, one on top of the head, and the other next to the artery on her neck. We administered Reiki right away, which instantly took care of the pain, the swelling and the reddening.

- We sometimes use Second Degree Reiki to bring peace and harmony to our classes. Once, out of the blue, two of our students started to beat and kick each, probably owing to excess energy. It started as a game, but soon got serious, and we had to interfere. We used Second Degree Reiki, and before we knew it, they were sitting together arm in arm sharing their snacks. It was a surprise for all of us. (I would like to add, at this point, that Reiki is not always able to turn violence into harmony, but it often does).

- I myself suffered from a periostitis (an infection of the bone lining) in my left foot for three years. I tried all sorts of therapies, including physiotherapy and ultrasound therapy to no avail. After giving myself daily Reiki treatments for several weeks, the problem simply disappeared.

- One of our friends, Mr. M. from Sapporo, gave his younger brother daily Reiki treatments for a broken arm. The doctors were surprised at the speed and smoothness of his recovery. The same friend works in a restaurant, and when he accidentally cuts his finger, the wounds often close the same day, again thanks to Reiki applications.

The following reports come from Mr. G., a chiropractor from Yamanashi prefecture, who teaches Reiki there since he learned it from us in early 1993:

- His mother once burned herself with hot oil on her right cheek, arm, foot and hand. She used her left hand to give Reiki to the burns on her right hand for 6 months and no scars remained. The burns that she didn't treat with Reiki all left permanent scars.
- Soon after she received the First Degree initiation from her son, she visited a relative who had been in bed for a while with a severe back problem. After a one-hour hands-on session (she spent 20 minutes laying hands on the patient's tailbone), the relative got out of bed, stood up straight and felt wonderful.
- A 50-year old client of Mr. G., who suffered from fatigue, chronic stiffness in the shoulders, insomnia, migraines and general physical coldness, recovered from all of the above discomforts after the First Degree Reiki initiation.
- One day, her employer was stung by a bee. His right hand swelled up and started to itch badly. After a few minutes of Reiki treatment the itching stopped. Several hours later, it started again, so he was given another Reiki session. The itching stopped again, and the swelling disappeared within the next 12 hours.
- The same person gave Reiki to a friend who was in hospital due to a neck injury incurred in a traffic accident. She had already been in hospital for two weeks without any improvement in her condition. After a one-hour Reiki session her overall disposition changed for the better, and she was soon discharged.
- Another client of Mr. G's., a 75-year old lady, was cured of her life-long constipation problem after the First De-

gree Reiki initiation. She practices Reiki every day for an hour, and before getting up in the morning, she always lays her hands on her belly for a while. Interestingly, her sense of taste also improved drastically. One day last winter she got frostbite on both cheeks. She gave Reiki to her right cheek only and woke up next morning to find her right cheek normal and her left cheek still swollen!

The Heart

Being and becoming

The only times we actually succeed in living in the here and now are during meditation or in moments of danger and surprise. When young, our minds tend to drift towards an unknowable future. We indulge in thoughts of becoming: "In a few years I will be rich and famous, happy and content, buy a new house, have children." Tomorrow, tomorrow, tomorrow. Becoming, however, is always limited because it leans on past experience. Becoming means postponement, and postponement means not living at all.

When we get older, we reverse the process and live in our past. We spend our precious present remembering moments long gone without realizing that all time spent unconsciously is not being put to optimum use. Consciously reliving our unresolved past can be a great help, but sacrificing the present moment with all its splendor in favor of the dead past is simply a waste of time. Instead of using Reiki for past or future events, (as explained in chapter "The Degrees"), we can treat it as our bridge to the eternal now. It is so easy, pleasant and refreshing to dive into the present moment while touching ourselves or another person. This very moment gives us total freedom, divorced from good or bad memories, daily fears, and future plans or worries.

Love

When I was a child, one of the worst things someone could say about another person was "he loves himself!"
I have talked to hundreds and hundreds of people from all over the world and all walks of life in the past 15 years and have found that everyone (including myself) has the same problem: We do not accept ourselves the way we are. Thousands of years of moral conditioning have built a seemingly indestructible cage around us. We have "learned" to accept our virtuous sides and to disrespect and even hate our darker sides.

We do not love ourselves in our totality.

With the help of Reiki we can learn to love ourselves again, and can use that love to tune into another person as well.

When touching others in a Reiki session, we meet them at a much finer level, beyond the body and its sensations, beyond the mind and its judgments. When working at this level, it does not matter who you are, what you look like, or where you come from.

This is the level of unconditional love. And there lies the beauty of Reiki and its attractiveness for modern beings. What we actually strive for in our lives is to find love and harmony, to reunite with the whole again.

In the depths of all our desires, be they "material" or "spiritual," we aim to return to that long-forgotten unity. We should remember this, whatever it is we are doing ...

Wholeness

One of the greatest calamities to afflict humankind during the past several thousand years, is its philosophical cutting up into three parts. The unity of body, mind and soul has been completely forgotten, yet without it there can be neither peace nor harmony in the inner or outer world.

The concept of oneness of macrocosmos and microcosmos is difficult to grasp intellectually- it must be experienced.

The human mind/ego thrives on dualism and constantly separates itself from the so-called "other." As a result, we have not only alienated ourselves from the rest of the world, but have also separated ourselves from "our own" body mind and soul.

Separation starts within our own body-mind system. We spend the bulk of our lives using our heads only, disregarding the other parts of ourselves completely. We do not feel our own body, or when we do, it's merely a tiny fragment of it. The following is an experiment that demonstrates this fact rather well: Take a piece of paper and hold it between your thumb and index finger. Ask yourself which part of your body you feel right now and you will find that you can only feel two fingers! By expanding your awareness, you will come to feel your entire body, a wonderfully intense moment.

Separation is, I believe, a disastrous disease. We separate ourselves from our fellow human beings and surroundings to gain individual identity. Even when we are together with friends or family, we set up high you-and-me barriers. The net result has been millennia of warfare and, most recently, horrifying environmental destruction. It's a heavy price to pay for individualism!

An easy exercise to enhance the sense of wholeness is to imagine looking down on the earth from a mile above. What we see is hundreds of people, greenery, mountains and rivers all in one perfect organic unity. The self-inflicted barriers of "individual" people with their fellow humans can no longer be seen because in the higher reality, they don't exist.

With regards to healing, keep in mind that cause and effect are inseparable. All is one!

Non-seriousness

The way I see it, Reiki can be a wonderful path toward a non-serious lifestyle. Seriousness is often mixed up with sincerity. Sincerity is a virtue but seriousness is a horrible disease, a cancer of the soul! With Reiki we learn to let go, to relax and not to manipulate or "do" things. To introduce a good dose of humor into our sometimes dry lives, I suggest the following three-step exercise, called laughing-meditation. It was described in an article by Sw. Prem Dhyan, a Dutch disciple of Osho Rajneesh:

Make a list of your favorite problems and laugh while doing so.

Then make faces and stretch your facial muscles for five minutes.

Laugh and/or cry for five minutes.

Be silent for five minutes.*

---

*For more information, see page 126

Meditation

I have repeatedly stated that Reiki is energy pure and simple. It has nothing to do with religion, astrology, New Age, psychology, personal growth, channeling, bodywork or even healing for that matter. It is we who give all these attributes to Reiki and thereby dress it in the clothes of our own choice.

Every Reiki teacher I have met so far does have a certain interest in "spirituality" not because of Reiki but in spite of it. Most of us have discovered our field of interest long before we came in contact with Reiki.

Ever since I was introduced to Raja Yoga as a teenager, my choice has been meditation. For me, the basic ingredient of personal growth is meditation: Without it all other "spiritual" fields are futile and can even lead us astray.

Reiki can be a very gentle introduction to the inner world of meditation. The time we spend treating ourselves or others can easily turn into a meditation if we do it with utmost attention.

The most common and easy meditation technique is observing our own breath. It's called Vipassana or "insight meditation" in the Buddhist tradition. It can be easily performed while practicing Reiki.

Here's how: Find a comfortable place to sit for 45-60 minutes. It helps to sit at the same time and in the same place every day, and it doesn't have to be a silent place. Experiment until you find the situation you feel most comfortable in. You can sit once or twice a day, but don't do it for at least an hour after eating or before sleeping. It is important to sit with your back and head straight. Your eyes should be closed and the body as still as possible. Use a meditation bench, a straight-backed chair, or any arrangement of cushions if you need support. There is no special breathing technique: Ordinary, natural breathing is fine. Vipassana is based on awareness of the breath, so the rise and fall of each breath should be observed wherever the sensation is felt most clearly, at the nose or in the area of the stomach or solar plexus, for example.

Vipassana is not concentration, and the objective is not to keep observing your breathing for a whole hour.

When thoughts, feelings or sensations arise, or when you become aware of sounds, smells, and breezes from the outside, allow your attention to go to them. Whatever comes up can be watched like clouds passing in the sky, you neither cling to it, nor reject it.

Whenever you can choose what to watch, return to the awareness of your breathing.

Remember, nothing special is meant to happen. There is neither success nor failure, nor is there any improvement. There is nothing to figure out or analyze, but insight may simply occur. Questions and problems may suddenly be accepted as mysteries to be enjoyed."*

Happiness

It is my understanding that all desires, spiritual or material, are rooted in the longing to be happy. We wish to buy this car and that house for one reason alone, namely the pursuit of happiness. However, happiness is a very elusive guest, like a shadow. The moment we think it is in our grasp, it takes its leave.

When a desire is fulfilled, another desire fills its place almost immediately. The carrot forever dangles in front of our face... We even use our desires to postpone happiness, saying "when I have fulfilled this or that desire I will be happy." The bad news is that happiness can never be found in the future. The good news: It is right here with us now at all times. Simply tap into the ocean of happiness by closing your eyes and looking within. At that very moment, everything is perfect, everyone is happy.

When asked by a disciple "What is abundance?" I heard my master Osho reply: "Abundance is when everything is perfect as it is." I think the state of happiness can be defined the same way.

---

* *The Orange Book* by Osho Rajneesh

The Body

Relaxation

Practicing Reiki is a great way to relax both body and mind, but it is not the only one. At this point, I would like to introduce two relaxation methods that I personally use and enjoy in addition to Reiki.

1) Progressive relaxation:

This is probably the easiest relaxation method. To relax a single body part, let's say the hand, tighten all the muscles in the hand as much as you can, putting all your conscious energy into this act. When it becomes impossible to tighten it any more, let go suddenly. This results in total relaxation. It sounds very simple, but it's actually quite hard to do if you want to do it well. The hand has lots of muscles that we are completely unaware of. We tend to maintain tensions unconsciously. By tightening each and every muscle and then releasing it, we can free ourselves of much accumulated unpleasantness!

The reason for tightening our muscles is that we have forgotten the language of relaxation. We can, however, attain relaxation by achieving a comparative state of tension. It is the same as defining darkness by light and light by darkness. Without the one, the other is meaningless.

This method can be applied for all parts of the body, but I believe it is easiest to start with the hand.

2) Autogenic training:

This is a technique developed by a German doctor, Professor J.H. Schultz, about 50 years ago. He worked in the neurological ward of a Berlin hospital and practiced hypnosis with some of his patients. He observed over a period of years, that many of his patients would feel a sensation of warmth and heaviness at the onset of hypnosis. He assumed that this feeling of warmth and heaviness was related to relaxation and then experimented with inducing warmth and heaviness in a patient's body without hypnosis. The result was relaxation. Normally autogenic training is divided into two grades:

The first one helps us primarily to relax our body.

The second one concerns the mind and gives us exercises to manipulate involuntary body-functions such as pulse. In this book I will just explain the first grade only. Second grade exercise should be learned under the supervision of a teacher.

The first grade can be performed by anyone at any place without any physical complications. It has two basic steps. In the first we learn to feel a comfortable heaviness in our body and in the second we feel soothing warmth.

Now to the exercises:
Lie down with arms stretched out beside your body, palms touching the bed/futon, and relax as best as you can. (It is best if you are not too tired because that could make you fall asleep during the exercise. Falling asleep would only set us back inasmuch as we would miss the exercise.) Just like in any sport daily practice is necessary if you want to achieve positive results. Once your body has remembered how to relax, practice becomes unnecessary or can be done irregularly. I learned this method when I was 15 years old to combat the stress accumulated in school. Now I use it whenever I feel like it, mostly while falling asleep at night.

Take a few deep breaths and say to yourself "I am completely relaxed." Then, if you are right-handed, say to yourself: "My right arm is comfortably heavy" six times. For left-handers it would be easier to use the left hand first, because it is "closer to he heart" (more ego identification).

Then repeat: "I am totally relaxed" and follow that with another six episodes of: "My right hand is comfortably heavy." Then again: "I am totally relaxed" and six times "My right hand is comfortably heavy." It's important to stretch your body gently after each exercise, wiggle your toes, play with your facial muscles and take a few deep breaths. Say to yourself: "I am totally refreshed, relaxed, and in good spirits" and let your eyes open slowly. For the next 15 minutes avoid driving a car or any other vehicle, and take it easy until you feel you are "back to normal." You may feel a little drowsy for a few minutes after practicing. If you don't feel the heaviness right away, don't worry, just feel your skin against the bed covers, feel the gentle pressure that it creates and you are on your way to success. It's also possible to imagine small weights or gravity pulling your body down in a comfortable and relaxing way.

If for any reason you start to feel uncomfortable during the exercise, discontinue it immediately, stretch your body, wiggle your toes, play with your facial muscles, and take a few deep breaths. Let your eyes open and say to yourself: "I am totally refreshed, relaxed and in good spirits".

Practice the first exercise for a week or until you feel it easily, then proceed and move to your lower arm (up to the elbow) for one week, then your upper arm for a week, always repeating the same pattern of 18 suggestions interspersed with the relaxation formula:

"My right hand is comfortably heavy" (6X)
"I am totally relaxed" (1X)
"My right lower arm is comfortably heavy" (6X)
"I am totally relaxed " (1X)
"My right lower arm is comfortably heavy" (6X)
"I am totally relaxed (1X)
"My lower right arm is comfortably warm" (6X)
"I am totally relaxed" (1X)

When you succeed in relaxing your right arm, move to the left hand. Then move to your right foot, right leg, and up to your right hip.

Then comes the left foot, etc. As soon as you are able to relax both your arms, change the exercise and use one command for each arm, not dividing it into three parts anymore. Do the same with your legs as soon as you manage to relax them both.

When you finally reach your head, change the "heaviness" to "lightness" since having a heavy head would feel uncomfortable. The second step is to first feel "comfortably heavy" in the right arm and then "soothing warmth," giving the following scenario:

"I am totally relaxed" (1X)
"My right arm is comfortably heavy" (6X)
"I am totally relaxed" (1X)
"My right arm is soothingly warm" (6X)
"I am totally relaxed" (1X)
"My right arm is soothingly warm" (6X).
"I am totally relaxed" (1X)
"My right arm is soothingly warm" (6X).

Now follow the same pattern until you have covered your body up to the solar plexus. Then suggest: "My solar plexus is streaming with energy (blissfully radiating energy)." When you reach your head say: "My head is soothingly cool" since no one wants to have a warm or hot head. It is helpful (but not necessary) to intersperse the above commands with a formula like: "Every time I exhale all tensions and worries leave my body. Every time I inhale more and more relaxation (or more and more warmth, comfortable heaviness) enters my body."

Most of us will feel the heaviness easily after a few days of training, but if it isn't felt after two weeks, just skip it and move on to the "warmth" exercise. Some people have an easier time starting this way around.

I know that you will be able to relax both body and mind quickly and effectively with this method. After 20 years of training, I can complete the two described steps in about 20 seconds.

This methods works very well when connected to Second Degree Reiki.

What Is Disease?

A basic human behavior pattern is to try to avoid pain and strive for pleasure. This holds true on all levels, be that physical, emotional, mental, or "spiritual." I have put the word spiritual in quotation marks, because what we usually call spiritual is just another, deeper aspect of our complex mind. The true spiritual sphere knows no dualism and therefore no problems.

Disease is a very complex phenomenon. It is a sign that somewhere along the line our energy flow is blocked or out of balance. It wants to show us that some part of our self needs attention and love. But because of our obsession with pleasure, we are not ready or able to look at it that way and be grateful for the reminder. Instead, we have learned to judge disease as morally bad. We try to avoid or get rid of it at all costs and as fast as we can. Many people both in Eastern and Western cultures believe that sickness originates in living in disharmony with their god's laws. In the West it's called sin and punishment. In the East we call it karma-accumulated deeds that can be rooted in previous lifetimes and have an effect on our present lives.

Guilt is another, mostly Western, concept that has unfortunately become associated to how we relate to disease: I have done wrong, received my punishment (in form of sickness), and now I will additionally poison myself with guilt feelings.

In order to understand disease and its messages a little better, we have to let go of our heavy baggage first.

Let go of guilt, punishment, karma, the whole nine yards!

The next step would be to stop resisting illness and start to look for ways to bring body, mind, and spirit together again.

One thing we need to understand is that disease is obviously a process, constantly moving, changing, just like health. Our body rejuvenates itself day and night: Old cells die, and new cells are born. Nothing is final, no disease is incurable, and no one can remain healthy forever ...

Orthodox medicine often only treats the symptoms of disease, without looking for the roots of the problem. When we have a headache we are given a pain-relieving pill. Many physicians do not even try to discover the source of this headache (you might be spending too many hours in front of a computer, like I do, and the problem can easily be solved by taking appropriate breaks ...).

In case of a more important disorder we have an operation and the symptom is removed from our body! But the cause often remains and will eventually find another way to emerge. We must broaden our views on disease and find ways to treat the whole body-mind system instead. Reiki practice avoids isolating the symptom and treating it separately, but gives energy to the whole body with the help of the twelve major hand positions. This allows the body to heal itself. The fact is, of course, that we often do not know the cause of a physical ailment.

As Reiki practitioners, we only function as activators or channels for the universal life energy. Of course we can, if so inclined or experienced, intuit what is actually going on in the ailing body-mind/soul system. However, it is always more beneficial for the receiver to have whole-body treatment.

And remember: dis-ease and ease (health) are always one!

The Healing Balance

According to Indian yoga, the human body is supplied with *prana* through three major and 80,000 minor energy channels called "nadis."

Chinese sources speak of twelve major energy channels called meridians and eight minor ones. They are the basis for acupuncture and Chinese-style Qigong, among others. In either system, disease is seen as the result of an obstruction of "our" life energy somewhere in these channels. Disease, therefore, boils down to either an absence or an overdose of energy at one spot. In the first case, disease can be counterbalanced by bringing energy back to the place where it is lacking. Using that extra boost of energy, the diseased body can then heal itself. In the second case, the accumulated energy is spread over a wider area and thereby absorbed.

In fact, there is no healer. Your body and only your own body knows how to heal itself. The Reiki (or other) practitioner simply acts as a catalyst ...

Generally speaking, we divide healing into two types: magnetic and channeled. Magnetic healing is probably the most common method. We have most surely encountered it at some point in our lives. Mothers, for instance, use it all the time with their babies, even though it is usually a rather unconscious process. When our little ones seem to be feeling discomfort, we pick them up right away to hold and caress them until they feel better.

Magnetic healing means letting your own energy flow into another person; it requires no method, skills, or training. It is one of our instincts. The first thing we do after hurting ourselves is to touch that part of our body in order to make it well again. And we all know how soothing this can be.

Magnetic healing has one big disadvantage: if we do it excessively we drain our own energy reservoir, which can lead to an imbalance. Another problem is that we often catch the "bad" energy of the person we touch and possibly become sick ourselves as a result. This is one of the major problems for professional body workers, and practitioners of massage, shiatsu and acupuncture. Several magnetic healers I know destroyed their own bodies in order to help others get well, which is a sad twist.

If you use a magnetic healing method, make sure that you clean up your own energy-body after each session. You can use the following exercises to do so:

- Wash both of your hands with cold, running water up to the elbows. Go to the toilet, if possible.
- Kneel down and put both hands with their finger tips touching each other on your solar plexus. Exhale slowly but forcefully through your mouth while leaning forward until your forehead touches the ground. Repeat the procedure three times and then hold both of your forearms in front of your body at a 90-degree angle from your elbows and shake your hands rapidly several times. Wash your hands with cold running water up to the elbows. Go to the toilet, if possible.

We prefer the second method, but the first one will do if you are short of time.

As the name suggests, channeled healing uses energy other than our "own," namely universal life energy. This does not mean that after initiation a person starts to talk in strange languages or the like. It just means that he or she becomes a channel or vehicle for the universal life energy.

The advantage of this kind of healing is that it does not exhaust the practitioner at all. In fact, the opposite happens: Both giver and receiver are energized, making them equal to each other. No "bad" energy is picked up by a Reiki practitioner, because there is no drawing out, diverting, or dissolving of energy involved. In a Reiki session there is no place for "doing" in the classical sense of the word.

Channeled healing, like Reiki, does need training and a teacher* who can open your channel for the universal life energy. Once opened, the channel remains so for the rest of your life.

---

*A person may come across a healing method through other means than a teacher, but this rarely happens. When it does, it comes as a surprise.

The Magic of Touch

It is no coincidence that our first reaction when comforting a crying child is to hold and caress it. Unfortunately, we have generally limited the magic of touch to two situations in our lives: pain and sex!

When we begin our Reiki journey, we need to dissociate ourselves from this obstructive pattern that is so deeply ingrained in our collective psyche.

Pavlov, who discovered conditioned reflex, found that the human mind, like the animal mind, functions by always associating a certain past memory with a similar situation in the present, even if the two are utterly unrelated and the present situation calls for a totally different response.

He demonstrated this clearly in the famous experiment with his dog: Every time he fed his dog, Pavlov would ring a bell. As it sniffed the meal, the dog's mouth would start salivating and, hence beginning the process of eating and digesting.

One day, after conducting the experiment in the same manner for some time, he just rang the bell without feeding his dog, which brought about the same reaction: The animal started to salivate! The dog had "learned" to associate the sound of a bell with food.

In modern behavioral therapy and NLP we call this process "anchoring."

It usually is a completely unconscious pattern that we are made to follow without having a choice in the matter. But it can also be used positively.

Reiki is the perfect tool to help break our habit of associating both physical and emotional pain with physical touch (1. we touch our body only when it hurts and 2. we touch or hug another person only when he or she is in emotional distress or during sex ...)

Every time we start to treat ourselves with Reiki, we touch ourselves as if touching our child or lover and thereby learn to associate touch with love. Love for ourselves is the first and most important step. Touching and loving others is the second step, and they should be taken in this order.

Repressed Emotions

All body workers and therapists agree on one thing: Repressed emotions can and do get trapped in body tissue if they have been repressed over a longer period of time. Even in our languages we find expressions that describe this process: "to swallow something," "to have cold feet," or "to get something off your chest."

Of course, it would be ridiculous to reduce every disease to a repressed emotion, it is just one possibility or one aspect of a very complex process. Constant questioning and searching for the cause of disease can be a disease and stress in itself! However, we often find that while receiving a Reiki treatment, a client may start to laugh, cry, or experience catharsis out of the blue without any visible reason. The practitioner should then give the client all the time and space to go through this experience peacefully, making sure that neither the client nor others are injured.

Afterwards it may be good to talk about what happened, if the client wishes to do so.

Our responsibly as Reiki practitioners lies in learning to tune into our clients on all levels!

It certainly is our responsibility to tune into our own body. Many years ago I talked about the matter to my friend Shankara from Switzerland, who is a wonderful healer. He suddenly said to me that my wife and I should exchange healing sessions while we were healthy, a thought that was revolutionary to me at the time. I had always thought of healing only in terms of or in connection to disease. If we realize that our bodies are usually loaded with minute tensions and repressed emotions at all times, the boundaries of so-called "health" and "sickness" disappear, preparing the way for a deeper understanding of our body-mind structure.

Suggestions

When you become interested in Reiki, I suggest you deepen your knowledge of anatomy and how the human body works. The easiest step is to obtain an atlas of anatomy. I spent all my time in biology class fast asleep, but when I bought an anatomy atlas I was so thrilled that I couldn't put it down. I literally shouted with wonder when I found out what a miraculous vehicle our body really is.

I also think it is a good idea to start being attentive to what you eat, drink, read, think, feel, say and do. An old Indian proverb states, you become what you eat. I'd like to add: You also become what you think and what you put a lot of energy into!

Personally, I have not found coffee, cigarettes, or alcohol to be detrimental to Reiki or any other energy work. In fact, the most powerful healers I know all smoke and drink! However, your body might have certain likes, dislikes, difficulties, or deficiencies and it's certainly worthwhile finding out about them.

It may be very interesting to discover what foods you are "addicted" to. Just a few month ago I was told by my friend Neehar that if your digestive system is not working properly, like mine, it might be helpful not to drink coffee and alcohol, and to avoid chocolate. When I quit the latter, I suddenly realized I had been addicted to it since childhood. The desire to eat chocolate crossed my mind several times a day for a couple of months, and I actually had very uncomfortable withdrawal symptoms!

I like to experiment with my habits in order to exercise my willpower and strengthen my awareness, but this is not everyone's calling. If you are in doubt about your food intake please consult a dietitian.

Severe detoxification methods like fasting should only be done under the supervision of a certified health practitioner.

Please don't take the suggestions in this chapter as rules. What I am trying to say in essence, is that it helps your overall well-being if you treat your body as well as possible. Healthy food, light daily exercises like walking, bicycling, or swimming, and drinking at least two liters of water a day will keep you in shape. Your body and mind will be grateful to you!

The Mind

Affirmations
and How to Create Your Own

The subconscious mind cannot distinguish between fact and fiction, so it is very easily manipulated by hypnosis, NLP, or autogenics. The language of our subconscious consists of images, so if we want to influence the deeper layers of our mind we will need the help of our imagination. That usually requires some preparation, meaning training, since modern humans in the Western hemisphere mostly use the rational part of their brains, predominantly the left side.

Our brains are divided into two distinctive parts, the right brain and left brain. The right side of the brain is responsible for intuition, art and imagination. The left side is for logical thinking, rules, and comprehension of systematic structures like syntax in languages. To train the right side, we should interrupt serious left- brain activities every hour or two and paint, play music, or just relax to switch from one to the other. We can also incorporate the right side into our learning process by using all of our senses. When studying vocabulary for instance, it would be helpful to imagine, visualize, feel, smell, taste, touch, or hear the sound of the object being studied. This improves efficiency. You will be surprised how much can be learned by this method without stress.

There are several exercises that can help synchronize both brain halves. One is to draw the symbol for infinity (an eight lying on its sides) with one of your fingers for a few minutes. Another is to do the same thing using only your eyes. A third is to draw the same pattern with fingers and eyes simultaneously. Another method to synchronize left and right brains, and at the same time train your imagination, is to close your eyes and imagine the letters of the alphabet above your left eye one by one, while at the same time imagining the numbers 1-26 above your right eye. If you are not familiar with the Roman alphabet, you can use any kind of characters in connection with the numbers 1-26. It is difficult at the beginning, but after a while it becomes almost automatic: a-1, b-2, c-3, and so on. After you have completed the alphabet once, switch sides and start again, this time with 1-a, 2-b, 3-c. Try it with capital, lower-case, printed and handwritten letters. You will notice that some characters and letters are easier to visualize than others. I practice this exercise in the bathtub...

Any system that works with auto-suggestion can be successfully combined with the Second Reiki Degree. Of course, affirmations cannot elevate you into spiritual enlightenment but they are a great tool to deal with psychological hang-ups and fixed beliefs. They prove to be very effective in making us more sane and our lives more enjoyable. They can be used to deal with issues like anger, jealousy, weight problems, drinking or drug habits, and the like: in short, the whole spectrum of human miseries.

The best way to understand how our human subconscious works is to study one of the afore-mentioned methods, which means studying your own mind.

It is very easy to create your own affirmations or auto-suggestions, but there are several guidelines to be followed.

The first is: All affirmations need to be formulated positively. "No's and don'ts" result in the opposite effect. Our subconscious translates words into pictures instantly. If I say to you: "Please don't think of a pink elephant," a pink elephant will most likely appear before inner eye for a moment. Strong words such as "success" or "cancer" sink in easily. Beware! Our subconscious reacts strongly to repetition, so use only words that invoke comfort and well-being within yourself.

The second admonition is: All affirmations are to be phrased in your own words and mother tongue (since most of our traumas originated in early childhood) for the optimal effect. Of course, they can also be in your second language if it's what you use primarily.

The third is: Only one affirmation should be worked on at a time, let's say over a period of three weeks. Then the next one can be focused on. If you already practice some kind of relaxation or meditation method, use it to calm down for 10 or 15 minutes before doing your affirmations. Self-suggestion works best when your mind is quiet and relaxed.

If you are not familiar with any method, just relax as best as you can and proceed with the affirmation technique described in the chapter on the Second Reiki Degree.

Use and Misuse

Reiki is safe to use in any situation with people, plants, animals, objects, or past and future events, but it is no substitute for professional medical treatment. In many countries massage or (psychic) healing sessions can only be given by certified medical practitioners licensed by the state. If you are not one of these, find out what the specific laws in your country are before offering your services. In Japan, "healing" can only be administered by a doctor or professional acupuncturist, massage therapist, chiropractor, or the like, without a license it is against the law to perform "healing" sessions for money.

Reiki can easily be combined with regular or alternative healing methods and, generally speaking, it cannot be misused. We do not own Reiki or great healing-power. It's the other way around. Without Reiki there would be no life in the universe since this force is its very heartbeat. With Reiki what is supposed to happen happens, and we are just a tiny little part of its benign organism. However, playing a small part does not necessarily mean being passive. With the help of Reiki, we can activate dormant energies and direct them to parts of our self, others, or our surroundings that are energetically blocked.

The ego enters our lives from all dimensions and all directions, not only in situations that are obviously "great" or "virtuous." We often turn our miseries into ego trips as well, so that we can hold on to them. Out of fear of change, we come up with assertions like: "I am the saddest person in the world" or "No one is as sick as I am." This attitude cuts off any chance for change.

I know several people who are trying to turn Reiki into an ego trip, showing off their great healing powers and walking on clouds. As far as I understand even this is part of life, and is therefore acceptable and serves a purpose, although it may be uncomfortable for others. It is a risk that has to be taken if our goal is to spread Reiki as a way towards a better world, one filled with love and care.

There are certain situations in which Reiki might be used as an excuse to avoid dealing with problems or interact with our fellow humans directly. For instance, if we have a falling out with friends or family it would be very easy to use the absentee method of the Second Reiki Degree to work out differences on the mental plane. But it would certainly be better to address the problem face to face with the other person.

My suggestion is to always question your own intentions before using the absentee method on anything or anyone. Once this takes place, we often see things in a different light. If we find out that fear or some other dubious motive guided our intention to use the absentee method, it would be better to find another way to solve the problem.

For Second Degree Reiki, I suggest you work only on people who want to be treated by Reiki and by you specifically, because it may make them feel uncomfortable to receive uncalled-for energy. The other person may feel manipulated. It has happened to me, and I did not relish the experience.

Reiki works best where want, influence, or active involvement are absent, so beware of being or wanting to become a great helper and healer. As a rule, you should wait to be asked for help. Helping and healing are secondary and nothing but a by-product of your own clarity. Avoid making them your priority. Of course, it is fine to offer your services with the above caveat in mind.

Reiki and Money

Let's face it: We all have hang-ups about money. Since money and dealing with it is part of our daily lives, I find it important to question all our preconceptions and ideas about this vital issue if we want to find a greater sense of balance.

Most of us are convinced that money is dirty and that in order to obtain it we have to sell ourselves in some way. It is said that money can't buy love and I say it can't buy Reiki either. At the same time, it cannot prevent either love or Reiki from happening!

There is no direct relationship between Reiki and money. Money is energy formatted so that it can easily and playfully be used by all of us for the exchange of goods or serv-ices. Money can be a beautiful tool, but the problem is our attitude towards it.

The one thing that always poisons our financial transac-tions with others is absence of clarity. In the case of a Reiki session or initiation, it should be clear beforehand what the "giver" would like in return for his or her services, whether that be a certain sum of money that feels right, or some other form of compensation. What other Reiki practitioners ask for their services should not be considered at all. This is an individual decision.

A very common misconception about pricing is that some-thing more or very expensive must be better than some-thing less expensive. That may apply to items on the su-permarket shelf, but certainly not to Reiki. Energy is en-ergy, it doesn't even care about the individual (not to men-tion the price) transmitting it!

On the other hand, human beings seem unable to accept and value something that has been given for free. The best example is our own body, our own life: It is amazing, how little we appreciate them!

In order to avoid the same devaluation happening to the gift of Reiki, Dr. Usui, after years of charity, started to charge money in exchange for sessions and initiations. He found that free Reiki treatments merely acted as a painkiller or sleeping pill for people, without challenging them to change and take charge of their own lives.

I assume that many Reiki practitioners, like myself, either discover or encounter the concept of charity within them-selves sooner or later. We want to be of service to our fel-low human beings and think that service must be given free of charge. Thousands of years of moral conditioning have created this misconception, but it seems that each of us has to learn it for him- or herself ... In some cases, Reiki can be passed on without compensation. Within your own family or circle of close friends, for example, the flow of energy is present anyway. It can be a beautiful experience for a practitioner to give Reiki to parents or siblings. In my eyes, the only condition for a free session or initiation should be whether or not the other person really wants to come in contact with Reiki or not.

Desires and Positive Thinking

In my eyes, there is no essential difference between "positive" and "negative" thinking, as both make use of the same process of hypnotism or programming. Through constant repetition we are conditioned by society and ourselves to think that we are good or bad, happy or sad, intelligent, or stupid ... Whether conditioned positively or negatively makes little difference: Our minds and lives are constrained, devoid of freedom to act and be in the present moment.

Of course, there is a difference between positive and negative conditioning as far as our physical and psychological comfort is concerned. Right from the start, we are taught not to be genuine. The happy child is rewarded, the sad child is made to laugh, and the angry one is scolded. If we continue along this path of emotional and intellectual dishonesty, our life is bound to be filled with agony and frustration.

From early childhood on, we are conditioned to focus on what we can't do or what we aren't good at. Indeed, if asked by someone to make a list of things we do well, our mind is liable to draw a blank. On the other hand, drawing up a list of inadequacies is easy. We feel comfortable about our shortcomings and at the same time we disrespect ourselves for them. The following exercise will reveal your own feelings about your abilities and inabilities:

Write a list of ten things that you feel you are poor at and a list of ten things others told you were poor at. Then look at the first list and ask yourself how you feel about each item. Be honest. Then look at the second list carefully and see whether or not you agree with it.

You may find things that make you angry or sad, things that you personally don't think belong there! You may also find something that you don't like about yourself and change it. As a child (and later), I was told I had a bad memory. When I did this exercise at the age of 30, I suddenly realized that this had been a heavy burden to me. I decided to learn a simple method of memory training, and within three months of daily exercise, my memory power tripled. If we truly want to change, change will come joyfully and easily.

Next, write a list of ten things you are good at and a list of ten things others said you were good at. The 20 items on these lists may open up new dimensions, they may even change your life completely. Most people find it much harder to draw up the third and fourth lists than the first two. If this be the case, go easy on yourself. Take a few days to write up the lists, if need be, but don't give up, you are worth the effort! Repeat this exercise six months later and compare the new lists with the old ones.

Family, friends, educators, and each one of us, all seem to agree on one point: It is helpful to indulge in negativity, to look at faults and weaknesses with greater energy than to look at positive qualities. Almost all educational systems the world round are based on this attitude, and the collective unconscious of the human race believes it. I find it important to be aware of both our talents and limitations in order to better understand our psychological make-up and thereby become integrated and sane human beings.

World religions teach us to suppress our desires and have labeled them as "bad." But even thousands and thousands of years later, we have still not yet rid ourselves of our dreams, and I am sure we never will, even if we keep trying to suppress them. It's simple physics: If you push a ball under water, it will remain submerged as long as you apply pressure, but will reemerge the moment you either loose your concentration or let go of it. Suppression is not the right tool! There is nothing wrong with desire as such, it is a natural phenomenon. Of course, desiring something other than what is right at the present moment and spending lots of time and energy pursuing it in our minds, is simply a waste of precious time.

To deal with our desires successfully, we must first understand them fully, which means tracing them back to their origin. A desire is never just the thing or situation desired. It usually has a deeper root, which must be discovered in order to take the wind out of its sail. Take the desire for money as an example: If you follow it back in time, it will lead you to the most basic human instinct, which is the fear of starvation. For anyone living in an industrialized country, this ruling concept is absolutely ridiculous.

Before using Second Degree Reiki on your desires, first dwell deeply on them and then decide whether or not to proceed. Many a desire will just wither away on closer inspection. I have heard someone say that the power of Reiki can make all personal desires come true. First, this is not true, and secondly it is not the purpose of Reiki and our spiritual growth to blindly follow absurdities and wish for their manifestation. The key lies in understanding and trust that all our needs will be met by existence.

Reiki and Channeling

Channeling as such has nothing to do with Reiki. With Reiki we channel universal life energy, not entities, gods, or spirits. In order to channel Reiki energy, no preparation other than the Reiki initiations is necessary. The mind is neither a necessity nor an obstacle. To be more specific: it does not matter whether or not our minds are wandering around while we administer Reiki to another person. The channeled energy flows regardless of personality, individuality and emotional or intellectual activity.

For clear channeling of "entities" to take place, the mind of the channeler must be absolutely empty, i.e., devoid of personal thought and memory. It demands of the channeler a state of, at least temporary, egolessness! If that is not the case, it will be almost impossible to distinguish between truly channeled material and undigested desires stemming from the subconscious of the "channeler" or the collective unconscious of the human race. Bodiless souls do not transfer words in a certain language to the channeler since they are free of language and nationality. The "feeling" or "truth" that is being channeled needs to be "translated" by the channeler without being polluted by his or her own unclear mind or memory. The path of channeling is a razor's edge.

None of the Reiki degrees will turn the practitioner into a channeler, if that is not his or her destiny.

Should channeling happen to you, I suggest you do daily grounding exercises (like those explained in the chapter on Reiki Two), Tai Chi, or Taoist breathing exercises, go for long walks in nature, and do at least 30-60 minutes of hard physical work or physical exercises every day. It would probably be best, too, to find a spiritual master to verify your experience or at least find a true and experienced channeler to help you on your way.

Coma and Death

Reiki also offers us a wonderful way to communicate with comatose or dying patients whose consciousness has apparently become inaccessible temporarily. With the help of the Second and Third Degree Reiki symbols, we can communicate freely with people who are unreachable under normal circumstances, leaving us fulfilled and grateful instead of frustrated and wrought with pain and pity.

At first I suggest that you match the "patients" breathing by exhaling and inhaling at the same speed and in the same pattern. This brings about a subtle and intimate feeling of familiarity with the other person on a deeper level. Then use the Second Degree symbols to connect with the patient on the mental level. At this point, there are several ways to proceed.

1) Mental healing:
If the person is still conscious, use the deprogramming technique described in the chapter on "The Second Degree" to help them make their transition more peacefully. However, it is also possible to do this with an unconscious patient by either using an affirmation made with the patient beforehand, or just making one up that is devoid of your own desires for example: "I am totally relaxed and filled with joy."

If we know the dying person well, it will be easier for us to come up with an affirmation that matches his or her character. It is best to say the affirmation while the patient exhales. It has been my personal experience that I seem to become involved in a silent dialog each time I meet a comatose or dying person after I have made contact to him or her through the Reiki symbols. I am usually surprised at what I "say" to the person and equally at their "reply."

My wife's experience is totally different. She doesn't converse with the patient at all, but just feels that whatever she may be doing (mental or physical healing) is deeply appreciated by the patient and a source of joy and courage to face what may well be the last moments of life and then beyond.

One of her uncles passed away recently and every time we left the hospital after we had given him Reiki sessions, we both felt very elated. Her uncle's health improved drastically after each visit. In the end he made a peaceful transition.

At the funeral and in the crematorium we again used the Second Degree symbols to make contact with him and so we could say good-bye. We felt very lucky to have had the chance to use Reiki in the final stages of his life.

I had seen many bodies being burned during the three years I spent in India living at the Osho Commune International in Poona, and I always thought it to be a beautiful custom until I saw the first cremation here in Japan. It seems that the fear of death has driven us to create a super-efficient, automated factory system to dispose of our dead in such a way as to avoid feeling anything at all. The Reiki symbols can work miracles when it comes to reintroducing some celebrative energy back to the sterile atmosphere of a modern cremation.

2) Physical healing:

To make someone who is suffering great pain or fear feel a little better, start by making contact through the Second Reiki Degree symbols. Then proceed by either giving an absentee healing session or an actual hands-on session.

In general, if the patient's breathing is a little heavy at first, it will slow down and deepen within a few minutes. If the person is suffering severe physical pain, it may be helpful to avoid touching the body at all while administering Reiki. My experience has shown that holding one hand on or over the solar plexus and the other on or above the top of the head for about 10-15 minutes is very soothing for the patient.

I would like to close this chapter by saying that it is not possible to bring someone whose time has come back to life with

Reiki, and it is not our business to attempt to do so. We will have to learn to accept death as part of this great big mystery that we are living, celebrating it as completely as we can.

Honesty

The ego believes in the advantages of dishonesty. Thinking itself alienated from the whole, it tries to manipulate life for its own personal good and possibly others' misfortune. Duality or its illusion takes its toll. Once we look at the "other" with burning intensity, imaginary borders disappear, and we are left looking at ourselves in the mirror of the "other." So honesty is not really an external value but an inner state of lovingness.

If honesty originates from guilt or fear, it is absolutely worthless and not a quality at all. There is an old Zen story to illustrate this point:

Two monks were about to cross a river, when they came across a beautiful woman who couldn't get across on her own. Breaking his vows, one of the monks carried her across on his shoulders. The other one was shocked but kept his anger to himself until they reached their destination. He complained to the first monk by saying: "You broke the rules and I will have to report this to the abbot of our monastery." To this the first monk replied: "I left the woman at the river, but you are still carrying her now!"

Awareness purifies all actions.

The Ego

A monk asked Joshu: "Does a dog have Buddha nature?" Joshu answered "Mu!" (Chinese for neither yes nor no). The same answer might be appropriate for the question: "Does the ego exist?" What exactly is this mysterious force, the ego? It is one of the voices within us that is constantly trying to separate itself (us) from the whole (our fellow travelers and our surroundings).

It tries to prove itself better, bigger, more important, and even more spiritual than others! In sum, it is one of the big misunderstandings, so much so that some enlightened beings deny its existence altogether! However, for all of us unenlightened souls the ego does present a problem. It seems to be constantly in the way of peace, silence and bliss.

The best way to understand the ego and its workings, as far as I can tell, is the art of meditation. Groups, books, workshops and methods all dealing with meditation are readily available. The interested reader can surely find what is helpful to him or her.

Independence

One major topic that has been rearing its head throughout the planet ever since the 1980s is so-called "independence". In Bosnia Muslims want to be independent. The component parts of the former Soviet Empire are all striving for it, Ukraine, Chechenya, Mongolia, Armenia, Georgia, to name but a few. What constitutes this desire for independence? I believe we are seeing the workings of unconscious desire for ego-centered power that usually arises from the collective unconscious.

If we investigate it closely, we will find that independence is a myth: Everything on earth and in the cosmos is interconnected. No man is an island. The tropical rain forests create enough oxygen for us to breathe, and the moon is responsible for the tides of our oceans. These circles expand throughout the universe, and I am sure that if we had more knowledge of the whole, we would discover that everything is inter-dependent, reliant on everything else.

Sadly, this factionalism has also struck the world of Reiki,; of course, this also has a positive aspect. Because this cancer shows itself so clearly, we can sharpen our awareness of it and discard it easily, if we want to.

As fellow travelers on the road to ourselves and a happier humanity, I urge everyone to abstain from falling into the trap of wanting to be "independent." I have noticed recently that in the field of business as well, things seem to evolve smoothly when work is done together. The days of greed as the sole motive for achievement are numbered.

Let's celebrate life and remember that Reiki belongs to all of us!

Esoteric Background

The Chakras
and Their Function

Most Eastern philosophies mention seven major energy centers or chakras that regulate the flow of energy in our bodies. The 12 Reiki hand positions are located "above" those centers and help the energy flow freely to and through the chakras for an individual's optimum health and well-being.

Physically, some of the seven chakras correspond to what is the most mysterious but still not scientifically fully understood part of our body-mind system, the endocrine glands.

The first chakra called *Muladhara* or base chakra is located at the base of the spine.

The second chakra called *Swadhistana* or sacral chakra is located 2-3 inches below the navel.

The third chakra called *Manipura* or solar plexus chakra is located in the solar plexus, just above the navel.

The fourth chakra called *Anahata* or heart chakra is located in the center of the chest.

The fifth chakra called *Vishudda* or throat chakra is located in the middle of the throat.

The sixth chakra called *Ajna* or third eye chakra is located between the eyebrows or slightly above.

The seventh chakra called *Sahasrara* or crown chakra is located a few centimeters below the top of the head.

These locations may vary from person to person. To verify the location of the seven major chakras in your own body, imagine energy entering your body between your anus and sexual organs. Then let it flow upwards into the region of the first chakra. When you feel it there, let it flow further up into the second chakra and so on.

If you don't feel a particular chakra, just keep moving upwards. Imagining the energy at a certain chakra is not helpful. Let it come naturally. This exercise can be done as often as you wish.

Following you will find a chart that explains the chakras according to their functions, corresponding colors, elements, gemstones, metals, endocrine glands, and perception of reality.

The Chakra Chart

The First Chakra

Color:	Red
Element:	Earth
Perception/Sense:	Kinesthetic, physical
Endocrine Gland:	Adrenals
Gemstone:*	Ruby
Metal:	Iron
Function:	Survival, prosperity

The Second Chakra

Color:	Orange
Element:	Water
Perception/Sense:	Feeling
Endocrine Gland:	Gonads
Gemstone:	Carnelian
Metal:	Copper
Function:	Physical health, sex

The Third Chakra

Color:	Yellow
Element:	Fire
Perception/Sense:	Emotion
Endocrine Gland:	Pancreas
Gemstone:	Sapphire
Metal:	Brass
Function:	Power, emotions

---

*The gemstones listed above are only examples. Any semi-precious and precious stone that corresponds to the color of a particular chakra can be used to enhance its function.

The Fourth Chakra

Color:	Pink/green
Element:	Air
Perception/Sense:	Love, empathy
Endocrine Gland:	Thymus
Gemstone:	Emerald
Metal:	Pewter
Function:	Love

The Fifth Chakra

Color:	Blue
Element:	Ether
Perception/Sense:	Communtion, hearing, speaking
Endocrine Gland:	Thyroid
Gemstone:	Turquoise
Metal:	Quicksilver
Function:	Communication, expression

The Sixth Chakra

Color:	Indigo
Element:	—
Perception/Sense:	Seeing, visualization
Endocrine Gland:	Pituitary,
Gemstone:	Lapislazuli
Metal:	Silver
Function:	Intuition, clairvoyance

The Seventh Chakra

Color:	White, violet
Element:	—
Perception/Sense:	Spiritual
Endocrine Gland:	Pineal
Gemstone:	Quartz
Metal:	Gold
Function:	Spirituality

The Spiritual Heart

The spiritual heart, also called the heart chakra or *anahata*, plays a central part in the spiritual evolution of human beings and deserves special attention. The heart chakra is where intense change takes place: It's where we move from ego centeredness to love. Located in the center of the chest, it transforms all energies from the lower and higher chakras into healing energy.

Reiki energy enters the body of a practitioner through the crown chakra regardless of whether symbols are being used. From there it flows to the heart chakra, where it is transformed. It then flows through two energy channels that run from the heart chakra across the chest out towards both arms. Descriptions of these channels can be found in either Chinese (Qigong) or Indian (Ayurveda) literature.

The energy then runs down through both arms into the two hand chakras and the finger-tips, from where it can be passed on to another person.

The Seven Levels of Consciousness

It is said that (human) consciousness here on earth manifests itself on seven levels or seven layers.

We usually refer to them as the seven bodies. Each of these seven bodies has certain functions that eventually help us achieve cosmic oneness. These seven layers of consciousness can show us fears and tensions that have to be counterbalanced on the way to integration. Generally speaking, fears and tensions are the result discontent with what is. They are always located in a nonexistent future. The ideal healing would involve letting go of everything except for this very moment on all seven levels.

The first body, our *physical body*, is the coarsest manifestation of consciousness. Its function is to teach us to be totally in the moment, to be aware of our physical form whatever we do: walking when we walk, and eating when we eat. We all know what the fears of the physical body are: disease, old age, death.

The second body is the *etheric body*. It has the same shape as our physical body but lacks solidity and gravitational pull. Many of our dreams are related to it. The etheric body can be worked on by means of mantras, symbols, incense and color therapy. Its function is to teach us unconditional love. Love with no boundaries, no limits and no conditions. Love that is not focused on an object and an outcome, but totally free.

The third body is the so-called *astral body*. It has the same shape as the first two bodies but knows no spatial limits. Hence the expression "astral travel." The third body is also able to move into the past, which is one of its limitations. Remains of past desires pervade the astral body, creating immense tension, which can only be relieved by total acceptance of those desires, whatever they may be.

The fourth body, the *mental body*, is made up of thoughts, as the name suggests. It is identified with our minds and the thinking process. The tension of the fourth body is confusion. We are forever thinking, one thought chasing the other for as long as we live. One moment we identify with being "this," the next moment we identify with being "that." The way to relax the mental body is by non-selective awareness, that is, observing your thoughts without identifying with them.

The fifth body is called the *spiritual body*. Its function is self-knowledge. The agony of the fifth body is what mystics have called divine discontent: We look inside ourselves, meditate and search for ourselves, but never find out who we are. The medicine for the spiritual body is silent meditation.

The sixth body, or *cosmic body*, is the borderline between ourselves as a person and cosmic unity. It is here that the ego clashes with existence for the last time in an attempt to keep itself separate from the whole. The way to transcend the sixth level is to let go of our individuality and merge with the cosmos.

The seventh body is called the *nirvanic body*, the source of everything. In this realm everything is gained and everything is lost, and one moves beyond existence as we know it.

The Collective Conscious
and Unconscious

As mentioned earlier, everything in the universe is made up of energy, energy of differing density. So-called matter consists of coarse and rapidly moving energy particles. Radio waves and magnetic fields are slower and finer. Our thoughts and emotions are even faster, finer and a good deal subtler. Nevertheless, they are made of the same substance as everything visible or measurable, namely energy!

One characteristic of energy is that it can never be create nor destroyed, as the saying goes, it only changes its form. Water turns into ice when chilled and steam when heated. And given time, a larva can turn into a butterfly

For millions of years, cultures have appeared, evolved and disappeared throughout the world. All the thoughts and emotions ever experienced by our ancestors are accumulated in a "giant storehouse" called the "collective unconscious. Every country has such a storehouse, albeit it differs from place to place. We mistakenly call it "culture" or "heritage," but it is in fact an involuntary "program," not unlike a bit of computer software. Once "possessed" by the program, the "victim" is made to follow certain behavioral patterns and no longer has the power to make decisions on the course of action. This should not be mixed up with destiny or providence, because the "power" of the collective unconscious can and does accidentally or consciously get suspended. There are millions of examples of unconscious behavior pattern acted out by each of us, as if we were in a trance.

For example, it is the collective unconscious that drives Japanese tourists travel to foreign countries in groups, not the inability to speak a foreign language. Traveling in tours enables them to take the Japanese collective unconscious with them from Japan to Hawaii, or wherever!

If we go to a foreign country alone, the collective unconscious of our own culture stops determining our actions and we feel either uncomfortable and unprotected, or totally free.

Having stayed in a foreign country for a while, a person starts to become adjusted to the culture and comes under the country's spell before adapting to it. When returning to his or her own country, the same game starts all over again. The collective unconscious of the country where a person has previously lived still has some momentum: this explains the hard time people have when they come home after having lived abroad for a number of years.

It also explains why many of us get hooked on traveling, the freedom from the pull of the collective unconscious is addictive. I myself traveled for most of ten years, always packing my bags just as I was starting to feel settled ...

Gurdijeff always stressed that we do not have a free will, we are simply forced to follow a certain cause until we become aware of our bondage. Sooner or later we are bound to encounter this obstacle on our spiritual pat. The first remedial step is self-awareness or the practice of some kind of meditation. After that, everything else falls into place.

As with everything in life, there is a counterpart to the collective unconscious as well, the so-called "collective conscious." This is the storehouse of collective knowledge. It is not a private or personal sphere. It belongs to all of us. The collective conscious is not, like its counterpart, dependent on specific locations on earth. It is always the same and is accessible in every country at all times. It is the source of information for the authentic channeler.

In his book *A New Science of Life*, the British scientist Rupert Sheldrake calls the collective conscious "morphogenetic field." He explains that everything in life, humans, animals and plants, are connected by this morphogenetic field, and that animals and plants always draw information and learning processes from it. He describes the results of scientific tests carried out in Europe during the 1970s to explain what he means. In one experiment, laboratory rats were let into a maze previously unknown to them. It took them a certain amount of time to work their way to the cheese at the exit of the maze, but they did learn how to reach their goal faster and faster.

The rats of the second generation were even quicker than their parents. But the best was yet to come: Similar rats succeeded in going through the same maze set up elsewhere very rapidly at first try. This experiment, which was carried out often and in many different labs, suggests that some kind of field exists providing information accessible to any rat on earth!

A similar observation was made with monkeys in an African country. One group started washing its fruit before eating it. A short time later, thousands of miles away in another country different monkeys had started to wash their fruits as well. The monkeys did not inform each other by telephone, they just shared the same information by tapping into the collective conscious.

There are natural healing systems all over the world, and some of them are very similar to Reiki. Polynesian and Hawaiian Kahunas use almost the same hand positions as we do in Reiki, so do some Indian, Australian, native American and Tibetan healers.

Reiki can be seen as a seed that was ready to sprout from the collective conscious, or the morphogenetic field of humankind by way of Dr. Usui.

The reason why Reiki has suddenly become so popular in the West in recent years, and now in Japan as well, is because it wants to make itself known to a large number of people in these destructive times. I estimate that the number of Reiki practitioners has reached about 700,000-1,000,000 worldwide already, and maybe you, too, will lend your hands in this chain uniting the earth.

The Initiations

In Reiki, the universal life energy is transferred to the student by the teacher via initiation. A Reiki initiation is an ancient way of transmitting energy from one person to another. Knowledge or understanding are not transferred in the initiation, just energy, pure and simple. Profound understanding of the Reiki system is something that comes with time and practice to the sincere seeker, it cannot be achieved through initiation.

Some Reiki teachers shun the word initiation, because it implies religious rituals, like fasting or various other cleansing processes, and call it attunement instead. Others differentiate between initiation as being the whole process and attunement as being one of several (in the first degree four) attunements. I don't see any real difference between the two, so throughout this whole book I have referred to the ritual when using the word initiation.

This word also implies a method, meaning initiation into something. Since time immemorial, religious teachers or masters the world over have used initiations to transfer energy or fundamental knowledge that could not be passed on to another person orally.

An example: Secret formulas, prayers, or mantras given to the seeker with a specific goal. Without the initiation the goal cannot be reached, in fact, some masters have said that it would be dangerous, for instance, to chant a certain mantra without being initiated into its secrets. Others have said that it simply won't work, and this is the case with Reiki as well.

The Reiki system, including the hand positions and all the symbols, does not work without initiation, since the channel for the universal energy has not yet been opened. That is why Reiki is so bathed in secrecy: It simply cannot be talked about openly with people other than initiates.

In the initial First Degree Reiki initiation, the Reiki teacher opens the channel for the universal life energy in the student. This helps him or her to absorb more cosmic energy for his personal well-being. With each of the following initiations, the process is intensified. From this point on, the Reiki student will remain a life-long channel.

The Symbols
and Their Esoteric Background

As mentioned earlier, the Reiki symbols are long-kept secrets that are passed on and explained to students by a teacher.

The concept of using symbols to direct energy and make it manifest is a strange one at first, although geometrical forms have long been known to have certain energetic properties. We have all heard about secret formulas, numerology and the great pyramids of Egypt and South America.

We are constantly surrounded by all sorts of energies, but we have forgotten how to use them. The discovery of electricity and electromagnetic waves has helped us immensely make our lives more comfortable. With Reiki we learn how to use energy inwardly, for our physical, mental and emotional well-being.

We can say that a Reiki symbol acts as a spotlight or activator to focus the energy of a certain quality on a specific spot. In a way, the symbol is or becomes this energy when used by an initiate. The intensity of the activated energy also depends on the affinity the Reiki practitioner has with the particular symbol he uses.

However, Reiki can not be used to manipulate situations or people, or to perform magic. Reiki is not goal-oriented.

The greatest magic is to simply be ourselves.

Much has been speculated about the esoteric origin of the Reiki symbols in the West, but most of the stories making the rounds are completely unfounded.

The actual word Reiki is not a household "term" in Japan. Our research has led us to believe that it comes from an ancient Shintoist mantra to protect the one who chants it. This implies that the word Reiki as such is a symbol (for protection)!

This mantra has been passed on from Shinto teacher to student by word of mouth for centuries, and we were initiated into it only after we promised not to pass it on to anyone.

The origin of the Second Degree Reiki symbols is confusing, because they appear in both ancient Shintoism, called Ko Shinto (translated: ancient Shinto) and ancient Buddhism. The power symbol and the mental healing symbol are slight deviations from the sanscrit originals. The pronounciation is Japanese. These symbols came from India to Tibet where they were copied by Chinese monks. From China they made their way to Japan.* The absentee healing symbol is derived from several *kanji.***

The Reiki Master symbol is an original *kanji*. It is Buddhist as well, and Reiki practitioners in Japan are not the only ones who use it for meditation!

Energy Phenomena

It may happen that our hands, spine, or chakras become warm or hot. We might start to feel things that we never felt before. Some might start to see auras, hear new sounds or smell new smells. Whatever it might be, it is only a side effect and should be understood as just that.

When we cook we do not focus on the boiling of the water, we just acknowledge it and keep going. If we get too attached to the phenomenon of "boiling," we'd never be able to fill our bellies. The same holds true for so-called "spiritual" or energy phenomena, if we pay them too much attention they will keep us from growing! Even great (and very ego-fulfilling) psychic powers are not the goal of our spiritual search. In the end the goal is simply to be ourselves.

Developing psychic powers, or *siddhis*, should be at most a "spiritual hobby," some spiritual masters even say that it

---

*Japanese Shintoism and Buddhism are so intricately intertwined that it is impossible to separate them. It is often difficult to say where one starts and the other ends.

**The Japanese word "kanji" is a character that was brought from China to Japan a long time ago.

can be harmful. There is an enlightening anecdote in the life of Swami Ramakrishna, one of the most profound Indian mystics of this century: He was once visited by an ascetic, who for all intents and purposes could walk on water. Ramakrishna reportedly asked the man how long it took him to learn the art. The ascetic, who thought himself great because of his skill, answered proudly that it took him 18 years. Ramakrishna laughed and replied that whenever he had to cross the river the ferry man would take him for only one paisa (less than one cent). "And you have wasted 18 years for one paisa?" he asked.

The Higher Self

This is the one word in the New Age jargon that always makes me grin. The Higher Self is said to be some kind of god-like voice or agency that talks to you, comforts you and gives you guidance once you know how to access it. I personally don't believe in this spiritual version of the Internet—it is simply your own subconscious that is "accessed," another mind game.

The concept of a super-ego has always escaped me: If we are honest with ourselves, we will discover that the longing for a "higher self" stems from not liking ourselves the way we are. Instead, we can begin right now to love and appreciate our very own self with all our strengths and weaknesses instead.

Here are some exercises that might help us on our way to celebrating ourselves:

- Look at your body-mind self as if looking at your lover/beloved, someone you appreciate in his or her totality. Unfortunately we have forgotten how to look at ourselves lovingly, but some of us still know how to look at another person that way. This technique attempts to reverse the process, it is a motion towards turning the arrow of love on ourselves. Whenever I see photographs of people like Ramana Maharshi, J. Krishnamurti, Meher Baba, or Osho, I am thrilled by the reverence they show for every living thing starting with their own physical form. The way they rest their hands on their knee with so much love and gratitude makes the rest of us look like robots.

- Be totally honest in your relationships. As we all know, this is a very hard thing to do, but if it is practiced rigorously it does produce self-acceptance. We tend to be afraid of hurting our loved ones with honesty, but the real problem is fear. And fear should never be a deciding factor in our lives. Being honest does not actually require hurting the other person, it just takes some courage to be oneself in the beginning. The first time I decided to tell my wife that I had had an erotic dream, it took me several hours to talk about it. And what a relief it was when I did and found out that she still loved me.

- Probe into yourself and make a list of ten lovable qualities you find in yourself. If you find more than ten, keep writing. When the list is done, go through it item by item every day for a week and truly appreciate yourself. The point of this exercise is not to hypnotize yourself by constantly repeating "I am great, I am great, I am great, I am great." This kind of affirmation is totally useless because we don't want to imagine anything, we simply want to see the fact that we are perfect the way we are!

- Allow yourself to be a strange person. If you do so, you won't have to fear other people's judgments.

- Find work that you love. If we spend our days doing something we don't enjoy, we work against loving ourselves.

Other Hand—Healing Groups

In his book called *Hands on Healing Techniques*, Tsuguharu Asuke states that about 20 different Shinto-based hand-healing groups appeared in Japan before World War Two. Most of them have disappeared since, but a few are still in existence. Apparently, what was then called "Nihon Reiki Gakkai" (Japan Reiki Society) was the core group of them all. Some people claim that it was not Dr. Usui who founded

Reiki, but a certain Mr. Morihei Tanaka, who belonged to a group called Taireidou. He was allegedly Dr. Usui's teacher. Since Taireidou vanished, however, it is impossible to verify this claim. We have not been able to find out exactly what Dr. Usui learned from Mr. Tanaka.

Other groups that survived the war are Mahikali Kyodann, Kyuusei Kyo, Omoto Kyo, Kurozumi Kyo, Konkou-Kyo and Tenri Kyo, to mention just a few. In the Kyuusei Kyo, there is a certain hands-on healing technique called Johrei. Some American Reiki teachers call themselves Johrei Reiki Masters. According to the Johrei fellowship in the USA, Reiki is not related to Johrei at all, and the two should not be mixed up. The following is an open letter that was sent to W. L. Rand and published in his newsletter of Autumn 1995.

The Johrei Fellowship by Ray Toba:
„The Johrei Fellowship is a religious organization whose main practice is the channeling of life force energy resulting in healing. The channeler receives the ability to do Johrei during an initiation ceremony. To do Johrei, the channeler sits in front of the recipient and raises the hands, says a prayer and the healing energy is transmitted to the recipient from the hands.

The Johrei Fellowship was originally incorporated as a non-profit religious corporation in the state of California in 1953 and is currently headquartered in Torrance, California with Johrei Centers and groups in many cities and states across the country. The principles and practices of the Johrei Fellowship are based on the teachings and philosophy of Mokichi Okada (1882-1955) known as Meishu-Sama to followers.

Okada taught that the cause of humankind's three great miseries sickness, poverty and conflict are spiritual in nature. He referred to them as "spiritual clouds." He further explains that these spiritual clouds could be eliminated through practice of Johrei, natural farming and the appreciation of beauty. While there are some similarities between Johrei and Reiki, it is important to note that there is no connection between Johrei and any form of Reiki. It has come to our attention that something called Johrei Reiki is being taught and practiced by people advertising themselves as Johrei Reiki Masters.

We have also learned that other Reiki Masters have discussed Johrei, Johre, and/or Johrei in written materials, including books, pamphlets, flyers and brochures ... There is also a symbol in use called Johre. All these terms are misuse of the word Johrei. Johrei is a sacred practice and the sacred name of our religion. Please do not use it improperly or connect Johrei with any form of Reiki ..."

My friend Ms. Lynn Wakisaka-Evans suspects that Kyuusei Kyo and the *American Johrei Fellowship may* have originated from the same source since both of them teach the Johrei method, but this is still being researched.

I personally find it very possible that some of Dr. Usui's students were either part of one of the above groups or started their own group after being initiated into Reiki. Japan is a land of synthesis and bootlegging. Copyrights are constantly being trampled on, and Reiki is no exception. One of our Reiki students asked my wife seriously whether he could give Reiki his own name, to which she replied that it seemed strange to have the desire to call "coffee" "tea!"

Another of our "students," who works for a large seminar company in Tokyo, says in his Reiki advertisements that he learned Reiki in India instead of Sapporo.

The human ego works the same way all over the earth, and whether we like it or not, purity cannot be found on the outside, it is the treasure of our heart.

Mount Kurama

Mount Kurama, where Dr. Usui received his Reiki initiation, is situated at the northern end of Kyoto. For centuries it has been known to be an auspicious place, a power spot. There is an ancient Buddhist temple on Mount Kurama that some people link directly with Reiki. This temple is part of the so-called "Mikkyo" sect, which has its roots in Tibetan Buddhism.

The temple was inaugurated in AD 770. During its 1200-year history it burned down eight times* (Reiki Fire) and

---

*Japanese shrines and temples are built of wood.

Main hall of the Kurama temple

Stairs leading to the Kurama temple

above: Kurama-Waterfall

left: View from Mount Kurama

116

was flooded once. In 1974, an enormous water tank was finally constructed to fight any further fires. Kurama Temple houses many artifacts that are part of the "National Treasure," the most important piece is a statue of Vishamonten, which saved from a fire that completely destroyed the temple in 1238. The noble and the powerful cherished Kurama Temple as their spiritual refuge.

Several Japanese Emperors came here frequently to pray and ordered the temple officials to keep the mountain and its forests in their natural state. The mountain itself is the spiritual symbol of Kurama temple.

The basic postulate of the philosophy of Kurama temple is called *sonten*, which translates as universal life energy, thought to be the source of all creation. It is an absolute truth and transcends the differences between all religions. It permeates the whole universe and, of course, humankind. *Sonten* shows itself on earth in three main manifestations: love, light and power. It is made up of this trinity, but each of its component parts include the whole within themselves.

The principle of love corresponds to the moon. Its spiritual patron is one of the manifestations of Buddha called Senju Kanzeon Bosatsu (Avalokiteshvara in India). Light corresponds to the sun. Its patron is called either Vishamonten, Bishamonten or Tamonten (Vaishravana in India).* Power is symbolized by the earth and is represented by Gohomaoson. Gohomaoson is the original deity of the Kurama temple and is said to have come from Venus six and a half million years ago. This trinity (love, light, power) forms Sonten. Sonten is also the name given to what we know of as the mantra of the Reiki Master Symbol.**

If you live harmoniously in love, light and power, you will find happiness. You will understand that existence takes

---

*There is only one corresponding sound for "vi" or "bi" in Japanese.

**In this philosophy I see a clear resemblance with the teachings of G.I. Gurdjieff and P.D. Ouspensky, who claim that one of the main principles that govern our planet Earth is the so-called law of three. In their system existence needs an equilibrium of three forces, positive, negative and neutral, in order to function harmoniously. These three forces are neither good nor bad, but simply complimentary. I find it very interesting to look at the Reiki symbols in this light as well.

care of everyone and everything as a mother tends to her children. Find harmony and love in yourself and learn to appreciate the universal life energy in everything.

Kurama philosophy teaches us three guidelines to live by, applicable to both the inner and outer world.

The first one is: Don't do or say anything bad, and work on yourself. This also means not to do anything harmful to your own body, mind and heart.

The second one: Be honest and work for the good of humanity.

The third one: Immerse yourself in the universal life energy and trust this source unconditionally.

If many people live by these guidelines, the light will spread all over the world.

Since ancient times there have been two ways to embrace this philosophy of universal life energy at Kurama temple. One way is by taking part in a religious ceremony there; and the other one involves initiation by the head priest of the temple. Anyone regardless of creed, religion, or nationality can be initiated into the secret doctrine of Kurama temple provided you are ready to dedicate your total energy to spiritual growth. It is not necessary to renounce your native religion. The universal life energy will provide power, insights and light no matter which path you travel on.

Learning
and Teaching

Teacher or Master

Western cultures do not understand the concept of the student/disciple, master relationship. For thousands of years the Western mind has been shaped by its morals, its languages and religions to continuously question, analyze and rationalize everything experienced or heard. Surrendering to another living person is absolutely out of the question. The word guru ,for instance, although a term of deep respect in Asian countries, is used as an insult in the West! This thought, followed to its logical conclusion has tremendous consequences.

In the East, the situation is almost diametrically opposite. In Japan, for example, everyone who has some kind of skill and demonstrates it openly is called *sensei* (teacher) respectfully. The master title is not so easily available. A master is someone who has mastered himself, someone whose spiritual journey has come to continuous fruition. It has nothing or very little to do with skill or profession. There are only two ways to receive the master title. Either the students/disciples of a teacher call him master out of their vast respect, or a student/disciple is given the master title by his master after having mastered himself. For that reason, many Reiki teachers like myself don't call themselves master in order to avoid misunderstandings. Mastery cannot be achieved or received in any way.

Learning and Teaching

There are only two requirements for anyone wishing to learn the art of Reiki:

1) The wish to do so and an open mind, a mind that is ready to learn. I find it important that the intention of learning Reiki be to learn it for yourself, as an investment in your own spiritual growth. Possible future teaching or business opportunities should be secondary considerations at best.

2) Finding a qualified teacher who is ready to teach! Having completed the Reiki system does not necessarily mean that someone will be a good teacher nor does it mean that the person wants to teach at all.

Obviously, the Reiki system cannot be taught within a few days, weeks, or months; it has been my experience that Reiki eventually teaches itself to the open-minded and open-hearted Reiki teacher. We advise our new Reiki teachers to start teaching only after they have understood what they have learned.

When I talk about practicing Reiki I do not mean practice for proficiency's sake. Reiki practice only helps us become an increasingly clear channel for the universal life energy. There is no doing involved at all.

Reiki energy not only adjusts itself to the specific needs of the imbalanced body when healing is administered, it also adjusts itself to the state of mind, the spiritual and psychological background of the Reiki teacher!

You will find that no two Reiki teachers are alike and this is the only difference between the one or the other. However, as I mentioned earlier, you will ultimately find a teacher who fits your needs. There are several different Reiki schools, some of which claim to be the only ones teaching the original system. This is a rather childish attitude. There is absolutely no difference whatsoever between the transmitted energy from one school or the other. The only slight differences are in the symbols and the initiation process.

Furthermore, all Reiki teachers are part of the same family and heritage, even if they are trying to separate themselves from the rest. Energy is energy no matter how you present it and what name you give it!

Where to Learn Reiki

Who is the best Reiki teacher for you?

On a finer level, all Reiki teachers are one since the Reiki Master symbol eliminates all separation. Technically it doesn't matter where and from whom you learn Reiki. You will definitely find a teacher who fits your needs. If you feel uncomfortable with the one whom you are learning from now, you can go to another one for the next degree. My feeling is that the relationship with your teacher should be one of trust. Where there is an open heart, everything else falls into place.

In general, it is better not to change Reiki teachers unless you strongly feel the need to do so. Often the relationship from student to teacher becomes one of deep friendship, so, if you can, let it grow!

However, if after your First Degree Reiki initiation you don't feel the energy clearly flowing through you, talk to your teacher right away. If that doesn't help, it may be best to review the First Degree and get the Second Reiki Degree from another teacher.

Several of our students checked us ahead of time by means of numerology, kineseology, astrology, or by using a pendulum prior to coming to learn from us, the possibilities are endless. If you are not familiar with any of those techniques, just trust your intuition, which is often the first impression you have of someone. Most Reiki schools or independent teachers will be able to either mail you an introduction or talk to you personally prior to making an appointment. Follow your heart!

Some of us may feel more comfortable learning Reiki in a larger group, others would rather learn it individually. Both ways are acceptable, but from my personal experience both as a Reiki student and Reiki teacher, the latter is preferable.

The intimate vibrations of a private initiation cannot be easily matched in a large group. However, this is just my personal preference. Also, I suggest not to let cost or location of a Reiki initiation be a deciding factor. It may be worth traveling a little further or pay a little more or a little less.

At any rate, a Reiki teacher, who says "MY" Reiki is better than "everybody else's" Reiki has not yet understood Reiki and won't be able to impart the spirit of Reiki to a Reiki student.

Reiki teachers who promise that serious diseases like AIDS, cancer, or mental disorders will simply disappear after a Reiki initiation should be avoided. I've heard that some people are in fact so irresponsible as to make these claims.

Some Reiki schools don't accept students who have already begun with another school and ask them to start from scratch (meaning the First Degree) again. Others, like us, don't care and just review the earlier degrees in order to iron out the differences.

From the depths of my heart I wish you a great deal of fun and good luck!

Glossary

Absentee method: healing method beyond both time and space.

Ayurveda: ancient Indian body-mind healing method.

Awareness: an unattached state in which a person observes his or her body, mind and emotions as if they belonged to someone else.

Catharsis: letting suppressed emotions surface, usually in the form of anger or sadness.

Collective conscious: storehouse of collective knowledge of humankind.

Collective unconscious: storehouse of collective rubbish like: fear, guilt, psychological pain, etc. of the human race.

Conscious: with awareness.

Chakra: a relay station responsible for supplying our subtle bodies with energy.

Channel or channeling: allowing cosmic energy and information to flow through yourself without obstruction of your own mind.

Duality: thinking in terms of I and you, always separating existence into this and that.

Ego: the mysterious force that separates me from you, often resulting in suffering.

Energy: electro-magnetic bio energy or life energy.

Healing: helping the body-mind back into a state of equilibrium.

Here and now: being in the present moment.

Initiation: in the Reiki system, the process of making another person into a channel for Reiki energy.

Intuition:	the sixth sense, knowledge that does not stem from past experience but is born out of the present moment.
Karma:	all actions leave an impression, an imprint, and ultimately have an effect on reality. The amount of effects resulting from this life and from previous lives accumulated by each individual is called karma.
Mantra:	secret formula usually given by the master to the student with the student's individual spiritual growth in mind.
Meditation:	a thought-less state of "no-mind."
Oneness:	realizing the unity and interconnectedness of the universe, including oneself.
Prana:	Sanskrit word for life energy.
Qigong:	Chinese methods used to achieve health, longevity and peace of mind.
Raja Yoga:	ancient Indian science of meditation teaching its students visualization and other mental activities in order to turn inwards. Raja Yoga does not make use of so many complicated physical exercises like the better-known Hatha Yoga does.
Session:	time spent working on someone's body-mind (massage, hypnosis, Reiki).
Spiritual:	concerning a deeper, internal level of existence.
Suppression:	not allowing either emotions or thoughts to surface, thereby pushing them into the subconscious where they work without obstruction.
Watchfulness:	Awareness

About the Author

Whether as an agricultural adviser in the hills of Oregon, a landscape gardener for Bill Gates in Washington, or a computer expert in New York, whether as a photographer or poet, Frank Arjava Petter, who has been a student of the Indian meditation master Osho since 1979, strives to perceive, shape, and heal inner qualities in the outer world.

At the beginning of 1993, he brought Reiki back to the land of its origin and started teaching the Reiki Master/Teacher Degree for the first time in Japan.

He currently lives with his Japanese wife in Sapporo, Northern Japan, where he heads an alternative language school and teaches various healing therapies and methods of meditation.

Addresses

Sw. Prem Dhyan, c/o The Secretariat of the Center in Favor of Laughter, Jupiter 1007, 1115 TX Duivendrecht, Netherlands, Phone 31-20-6900289

Open Sesame, Ferris Nishino Bldg. 2 F 6 Chome, 2 Jyo, Nishino Nishi-Ku, Sapporo 063, Phone: (011) 667-3161, Fax: (011) 667-3162, E-mail: opsesame@phoenix-c.or.jp

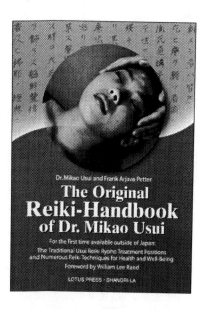

Dr. Mikao Usui and Frank A. Petter

The Original Reiki Handbook

The Traditional Usui Reiki Ryoho Treatment Positions and Numerous Reiki Techniques for Health and Well-Being

For the first time available outside of Japan: This book will show you the original hand positions from Dr. Usui's handbook. It has been illustrated with 100 colored photos to make it easier to understand. The hand positions for a great variety of health complaints have been listed in detail, making it a valuable reference work for anyone who practices Reiki. Now that the original handbook has been translated into English, Dr. Usui's hand positions and healing techniques can be studied directly for the first time. Whether you are an initiate or a master, if you practice Reiki you can expand your knowledge dramatically as you follow in the footsteps of a great healer.

80 pages, 100 photos, $ 14.95
ISBN 0-914955-57-8

Frank Arjava Petter

Reiki – The Legacy of Dr. Usui

Rediscovered documents on the origins and developments of the Reiki system, as well as new aspects of the Reiki energy

A great deal has been written and said to date about the history of Reiki and his founder. Now Frank Ajarva Petter a Reiki-Master, who lives in Japan, has come across documents that quote Mikao Usui's original words. Questions that his students asked and he answered throw light upon Usui's very personal view of the teachings. Materials meant as the basis for his student's studies round off the entire work. A family tree of the Reiki successors is also included here. In a number of essays, Frank Ajarva Petter also discusses topics related to Reiki and the viewpoints of an independent Reiki teacher.

128 pages, $12.95
ISBN 0-914955-56-X

Music for Reiki Treatments

Reiki: Light Touch
Merlin's Magic
One of the most recommended music for Reiki treatments. This beautiful, serenely blissful instrumental music is a real gift for healing and happiness. It's soothing sounds and caressing vibrations are wonderful for so many forms of body work, energy balancing, meditation or even relaxing. Combining guitar, keyboards, violin, viola and deeply resonant Tibetan bells to create the relaxing sounds of LIGHT TOUCH. 60 min. Inner Worlds Music
MC: ISBN 0-910261-79-2
CD: ISBN 0-910261-85-7

Healing Harmony
The Best of Merlin's Magic
Merlin's Magic is a proven best-seller. Now Merlin's Magic presents a wonderful follow-up compilation album to their best-selling former albums Reiki, Reiki Light Touch, Heart of Reiki and Angel Helpers. Also it presents two new compositions. This recording will delight you! Inner Worlds Music. 73 min.
MC: ISBN 0-910261-48-2
CD: ISBN 0-910261-50-4

Reiki
Merlin's Magic
Reiki Music was specifically composed and arranged to be played during Reiki treatments. However, because of its gentle, suggestive powers, it is an equally ideal background for other forms of bodywork and techniques of energy balancing. 60 min. Inner Worlds Music
MC: ISBN 0-910261-81-4
CD: ISBN 0-910261-87-3

The Heart of Reiki
Merlin's Magic
The Heart of Reiki comes from the deepest centers of energy to touch the hearts of listeners and create the perfect balance of body, mind and soul. It's a powerful celebration of the ethereal Reiki energy, more healing and more blissful than ever.
One long session of music that is sure to relax and calm while invigorating. Perfect accompaniment for Reiki treatment or body work sessions of any kind. 60 min.
Inner Worlds Music
MC: ISBN 0-910261-53-9
CD: ISBN 0-910261-52-0